MAKING MONEY
the Millennial Way

An Entrepreneurial Approach
to Getting Out of College Debt

By Abigail Widynski

SOVEREIGN VENTURE
ADVISORS

Making Money the Millennial Way by Abigail Widynski

Published by Sovereign Venture Advisors

760 N. Collier Boulevard, Unit 309

Marco Island, Florida 34145

Visit the author's website at www.getoutofcollegedebt.com.

Edited by: Tracy Teel, Finesse Writing & Editing.

Ordering Information:
Quantity sales. Special discounts are available on quantity purchases by corporations, associations, and others. For details, contact the publisher at the address above. Orders by U.S. trade bookstores and wholesalers. Please contact Sovereign Venture Advisors: Tel: (440) 361-0397 or Email: info@sovereignventureadvisors.com.

Publisher's Cataloging-in-Publication Data:
Widynski, Abigail.
Making Money the Millennial Way: An Entrepreneurial Approach to Getting Out of College Debt / Abigail Widynski – 1st ed.
p. cm.
ISBN 978-0-9863720-0-1 (Trade Paper) – ISBN 978-0-9863720-1-8 (e-Book)
1. Business. 2. Finance, Personal.

I. Widynski, Abigail. II. Making Money the Millennial Way.

First Edition: January 2015

Printed in the United States of America

DEDICATION

Thank you to my Father, who has graciously
brought me so far on a wild journey with so much
more to come. Your goodness chases after me.

And thank you, Dad. Who would have thought
the journey would pass by on pages?

CONTENTS

INTRODUCTION

Alzbeta, that was the name by which we came to know her, probably out of sheer necessity, or perhaps so that she would know we were actually addressing her and not some object in the classroom. After all, those were the days of sounding out e-a-c-h and e-v-e-r-y letter.

To the left of 'Intensive Czech I' written on that stapled syllabus, were a dozen or so consonants with the obligatory vowel or two. That's apparently what constituted a Central European last name. Syllabus in sweating hand, I vaguely knew which room I was to go to.

At the very least, the 'Dr.' part of her name meant something to our class, even if we weren't entirely certain about the gender of this professor. We were all out of our comfort zone, certainly culturally, yes even technologically!

The classroom wasn't the stadium-seating lecture hall with multiple screens and Wi-Fi to occasionally post a status update mid-class. Prepare to journey back with me a few decades! The classroom seats were completely wooden, the room equipped with a single blackboard, white chalk sitting on the holder and...

In the corner sat, presumably, the elderly professor. She leaned back in what was the only padded chair in the room. With one side of her mouth upturned, which I later realized is key to pronouncing those tricky consonant-laden Czech monstrosities called words, she watched us with ice-melting intensity from that first day.

Settled into the seats, we were a group of 12 that decided to take advantage of not only the language component but all Prague had to offer. We were a group of American students from all different universities united only by the choice to study abroad for a semester in Czech Republic. Looking back, I was probably motivated by survival. Those first few days of eating offered slim pickings for me, a non-Czech-speaking vegetarian, in a place I quickly realized was a meat-and-potato loving locale.

Alzbeta was our lifeline. While the other sixty students in the program saved themselves from a few more hours a week of language immersion, the 12 of us were in what was called the advanced or 'intensive' cohort.

Our new professor quietly stood, picked up a piece of chalk, and turned her button-down sweatered self toward the board. She addressed all of us, saying something none of us understood. She began to say her name over and over. This very first word, a name, was, I believe, the most important name we learned in Czech. She followed her introduction with an object lesson for life; a lesson on a day that created a vivid memory because of what happened next.

Now on a first name basis, Alzbeta asked us, in English, thankfully, to get out our wallets. We dumped our change on the yellowing laminate tables and sorted the coins by size. It must have been comical to watch from her eyes, rather like kindergarteners looking with wonder at plastic, fake coins during a lesson on counting money. 21 and 22-year-olds picking up each small piece of metal, looking at one side then the other with a mix of excitement due to the fact that money is a necessity in any culture and bewilderment, because we didn't understand the coins' denominations. Alzbeta started holding up each coin and repeating, again and again, the assigned value. With a generous exchange rate pre-Euro, we were thrilled to hear how wealthy we were. It was a matter of understanding the value: the value of what we had. Just because we didn't know how much each coin and bill was worth didn't make them worthless.

You see, Alzbeta didn't need to know that a woman named Sallie Mae, a savings-oriented Dad, or those paid weekend gigs freshman year paid the tuition for the program and the very pocket change we were counting. Money is money. Just because it's in a different form doesn't mean its benefit to us is diminished. (And you don't need a graduate-level economics course to understand the concept of purchasing power, do you?) Let me say it another way: The currency may have been different, but it still had value. It had worth, just like tuition payments.

This leads me to ask you a question. When you read the title of this book, what word caused a little spark? Was it the word 'money' or 'capitalizing?' Were you first intrigued by the word "millennial?" Or you, perhaps like me when I signed up for intensive Czech, were attracted to the subtle hope in the words 'starting now.'

If you honed in on 'debt,' I have a hunch you are not alone, statistically speaking! The numbers do the talking on how Millennials value education but also to the great extent that they 'put their money where their mouth is!' Did you know that 7out of 10 college students fold up their cap and gown after graduation and walk into their careers with educational loans?[i] The Federal Reserve Board of New York estimates that currently 37 million students, former students, and graduates are educational loan borrowers, and of that, over 15 million fall in the Millennial age bracket of under 30.[ii]

Just how much collective debt is there, both in arrears and in repayment?

Bloomberg reports that the collective indebtedness of former students and graduates has surpassed $1 trillion.[iii] The average debt load per student is now $29,400, up from $26,600 just the year before.[iv] The increase is undeniable, the scale ever-increasing.

But it isn't just the debt that's increasing, and this is where the 'chicken and egg argument' actually has a definitive answer. The trigger is the increasing costs of that undergraduate or graduate degree. Take, for example, a student going after an undergraduate degree at a public institution. The U.S. Department of Education reports that in 2011–2012 that student, on average, paid $14,300 for tuition, room and board, and books. Just 10 years earlier, that freshman would have paid 40% less. But what about private institutions and their students? Those starting out their undergraduate studies at a private university would have seen a 28% increase in tuition for those same fees from 2001–2002 to 2011–2012.[v] So how is that hike paid for? Or rather, who is absorbing the increase? We all know the answer: students and parents, through loans and debt.

College debt is becoming increasingly harder to pay off, according to the New York Federal Reserve Board. In 2011, 25% of student loan borrowers under 30 years old in the Millennial age bracket were past due on their payments. This same age group, representing nearly 40% of all borrowers, reveals an astonishing 3.6 million Millennials that couldn't make payments, even with their diploma in hand![vi] And the parents are watching, having never seen this amount of student debt.

It was a few of these such parents with whom I shared my intention to initiate a hope-begetting, solutions-driven dialogue around those startling statistics. After all, debt is part of my story and representative of our generation, yours and mine.

I quickly realized in these conversations that the term 'Millennial' isn't universal, but that the phrase, 'young people,' is more commonplace! However, for the purpose of our dialogue, I'd like to use the term Millennial. So, let's put parameters on it. *What or who is a Millennial?* According to Pew Research, a Millennial is anyone born between 1981 and 2000, which is anyone between the ages of 14 and 33 at the time of publishing, but there's some dispute to narrow that demographic. *Forbes* takes a more narrow approach in their headcount, citing that Millennials are the generation born between 1982 and 1993, putting ages 21–32 years old in the category. According to that measurement, there are about 80 million of us Americans in *Forbes'* designation of Millennial.[vii] (In case you're curious how many there are globally, a Viacom study cites 2.5B)[viii] But for our purposes, we'll opt to use the loose definition behind the name: Pew Research reasons that Millennials "are the first generation to come of age in the new millennium."[ix]

So given the collective and individual debt burden of our young generation, I think it's time to start that conversation about solutions, don't you? The conversation about debt and getting out of it sooner, rather than later!

In my initial conversations with Millennials and their parents, I noticed a number of head nods after establishing 'who' we are. The economy in which Millennials are graduating has substantially changed. After all, did student loans even exist when the parents of Millennials went to college? Non-government student loans didn't commence until 1996, after Sallie Mae was privatized.[x] This details the changes your parents and others see!

I also had the privilege of listening to these individuals share their time-enhanced perspective. Here is what I quickly realized: the issue of college debt is seen as the tip-of-the-iceberg, and some mindsets are labeling the generation underneath it. Here are some of the specific comments I received: "What about financial planning for these kids?" or "Education is all wrong. You shouldn't have to 'pay' to 'go find yourself,'" or "It's just peer-pressure to go to college nowadays!" Have you heard those comments as well?

That was the start of our conversation, yours and mine, in this book. Let me be clear: the end of the conversation isn't for me to publish this book and you to pick it up on Amazon. The goal is to get you out of debt quickly, and the process begins by asking some questions that will unlock your future, a debt-free one!

First, allow me to address the limitations of our conversation, so we're both 'on the same page.' This book isn't to address whether or not students should go into debt, because, chances are, the decision has already been made. You made the best choice with the information you had available, so let's not tarry. Here a few other things we aren't going to talk about:

-Which industry will be the most lucrative for graduates in the next decade?

-What the best cocktail of degrees for a specific career track is?

-Is student debt favorable in the long-term or not?

-How to decide when and how to acquire your education?

Remember that word that jumped off the screen or shelf in the title, "Making Money the Millennial Way: An Entrepreneurial Approach to Getting Out of College Debt? I'd invite you to think of that word, your "spark" word, the one that is already in your mind. I wrote this book with the word 'fuel' in my mind! It is my intention to use the fuel to spark your attention. My purpose for writing this book is to help you realize that you have it within you to succeed today because of who you are and how you were created. Certainly, I do not know you personally, but here's what I do know: You are here for a purpose, a purpose beyond paying your debt and a purpose bigger than yourself. That's something to talk about. And we will!

In the following pages, here's what you can expect:

- A new lens to identify money-making opportunities around you;
- A bit of humor and stories from students who have been there, done that;
- A solution to the challenge of balancing earnings and studies;
- End-of-chapter questions to launch you forward as you invest yourself in your future; and
- 25 opportunities broken down into three sections: 'The Idea,' 'Getting Started,' and 'The Nitty-Gritty of Pricing and Overhead.'

There's no time like the present…

CHAPTER I

THERE'S TUITION...AND THEN THERE'S RAMEN, PIZZA, AND BAKES SALES!

'Last one made, college paid... Time to go out –who's with me?'

Scrolling down my Facebook feed one day, I casually skimmed through the birthdays, the bad days, and other unnecessary knowledge. My mind was on what I call 'social media delay.' That's when your mind starts playing a ping pong game. Thoughts keep going back and forth but deep processing just isn't happening as you stare at your computer screen. Anyway, I was on 'social media delay' when I saw a post. I moved the page back up and read and then re-read it: Jonathan's[xi] update.

In that rapid-fire questioning only you can hear in your head, I said: *Did he just over-share, or am I just really private about my financial situation? Goodness, how long has it been since he graduated? Wait. Didn't we graduate the same year? He didn't seem stressed when we were studying together but obviously this debt thing being gone is a huge deal to him. Why else would he feel the need to broadcast something so personal? [Gulp.] Like student debt.*

Nine years ago, Jonathan and I sat in the same Intensive Czech class in Prague, bonding rather awkwardly over counting money with Alzbeta on that first day of class. We soon realized that we were round-the-corner-neighbors in the expat area called Vinohrady. Through our studies, we became acquaintances, classmates, and also co-travelers. (I still have a memento tourist picture taken in front of Schaumberg Palace in Austria featuring our pearly whites; pre-#selfie.)

Suffice to say, back then, as adventurous study abroad students navigating a new culture, we had shared some conversation about the cost of our program but nothing beyond that. It's said that time offers perspective, and I couldn't agree more as I sat in front of the screen thinking about the number of years that had passed, the vivid memories of a great experience in my life, and yes, money, or rather, tuition money.

Nine years. For nine years, he'd been paying for those four months and the rest of his education. Then it hit me. I had loans from the same exact time period. And I was still paying. I suppose we both learned a few things about money, such as its time value, during those repayment years. After all, just how many things do we learn by sheer experience? And for some, learning the time value of money comes through seeing auto-debit leave the checking account, monthly! That's the piece of tuition we pay for life, isn't it?

But money is money. Tuition is tuition, and it's certainly not always monetary!

Bonnie, a student at Consumnes River College, happily recounted on her timeline how she managed time to makes ends meet while in college. I say happily because she's now getting into her groove as a web evaluator!

> *"The first thing I did was look for paid internships. None of which panned out. The next thing I tried was [a gig website], but that was a bust because I was making maybe $10 per a day, if anything at all. Then I found [another gig website] which was a freelancing site where companies outsource different tasks that would take too much of their time. I made/make okay money. It's not going to do much for education funds... I tried $3 per an hour jobs or $20 for one time projects. Currently, I'm in the process of starting my own Virtual Assisting business. Since I'm not really making money...I decided to find other ways to make ends meet. Freebie trading and drop shipping are currently a couple of things I'm working on right now. No, they aren't 'get rich jobs,' but I won't be eating top ramen."*

You've likely heard countless more humorous tales of making ends meet, and the statistics tell the same story. Nearly 1 in 2 students "who took out college loans and are no longer in school, say repaying the debt has made it harder to make ends meet," according to Pew Research

Center surveys.[xii] It's not pleasant, to say the least, and if you're in that position, you're probably talking about it! (Notice, I didn't say that you were complaining because you made the best decision you could with the information you had at the time, right?)

Think about the advice you've likely been given by someone older when times have been hard. Maybe like when you were in a summer job with that horrific boss or felt as though your current "situation" would never turn into the dream job you wanted. Did that well-meaning person say something like, "Well, we all had to put in our time at one point or another?" If it doesn't sound familiar, count yourself blessed!

That well-meaning advice to 'put in your time' isn't very inspiring, is it? There is almost a sense of drudgery for work, isn't there? In fact, I can't think of more excruciating advice since it doesn't solve the problem at hand. It doesn't pay the bill that's due in three days; it doesn't make that co-worker start holding up her end of the job, and it does little to instill hope. Hope is music to our ears during difficult times, isn't it? However, hope seems a bit more realistic after a fresh, hot pizza is delivered to your door, pizza from, say, Domino's…

A few months ago, I had the distinct honor of attending a celebratory dinner with Domino's founder, Tom Monahan. After selling his franchise to Bain Capital in 1998 for $1.1 billion, Mr. Monahan exchanged his Founder, Chairman, President, CEO, and Chief Innovator hats for a few more: Education Champion, Pro-life

Advocate, and Philanthropist.[xiii] On this particular evening, we were a group of 60, honoring Mr. Monahan's work in South Florida for children and expectant women. After a lovely multi-course meal, it was time for Mr. Monahan to say a few words. Expecting to see an overtly confident man striding forward to a stage on which he's probably stood many times, I was astounded to see he commanded a different presence. I witnessed a man who walked with effort, and intentionality, and whose words spoke of his reality; hardship. Hardship?

Yes, hardship is in everyone's story. It's been said that it is easy to see the success and not know what path it took. I'd like to think that surviving, and then thriving through your 20s, is much the same. It was that way for Tom Monahan as well.

Standing behind the microphone and leaning on the podium, Mr. Monahan shook his head, saying, "We got a patent for the corrugated box because we couldn't keep the pizzas hot. Our first store was by a campus, and we were the first to deliver pizzas to the door. I was driving back and forth from store to dorm many times a night. I couldn't keep the pizzas hot."

But that wasn't the only challenge. For a man who admittedly had no business knowledge and who bought a pizza shop on a shoestring, 'putting in his time' meant doing whatever it took to survive and provide for his wife, whom he met when out on a delivery. There wasn't much time for deliberation. He needed cash every night.

Those were the early days, and as you know from your own late night dorm delivery, he created a nationally recognized chain of franchises from that first single store. He put his time in, right?

I would say he had. Internal problems arose over the years, though, the lawsuits kept stacking up, and two decades after getting the keys to his Michigan pizza shop, he literally found himself starting over from scratch, financially and managerially. His wife asked him directly, "Was it worth it to be back to square one now?"

It was difficult, but he kept going, building again and depending on others as well as his own skills. He remembered the years of having success, having problems that were sometimes solved, to the tune of some 100 patents. The patents weren't just numbers to Mr. Monahan. Each one was a challenge. Every time he had a problem, he created a solution. One hundred patents later, he had a plethora of solutions! Although that's true, and many would have given up, he "put in his time" by creatively solving 100 problems that saved his business.

On those late night deliveries when as the owner he might have preferred to hire out and let someone else do the delivering, he continued driving himself. That was his education. By showing up for himself, he learned to solve problems and overcome challenges. That leadership mindset became the education that paid him dividends throughout his career. Why? Because he understood that not all education happens in a classroom, just like not all tuition is paid to a college or university.

Once again, here's the maxim: tuition is tuition! We all pay tuition for life through our work. We always seem to work and work, never getting much closer to financial freedom or our dreams! But tuition simply can't be viewed as a necessary evil or a barrier to getting to where you want to go personally or professionally. Because, what is it really? Ideally, tuition is an equal exchange, a business transaction. When you decided to attend college, one of your motivators may have been to acquire knowledge that you didn't yet possess. So, you went in search of viable options to gain or buy that knowledge. That search is what bought you to a university.

A university sells a product that you don't have but want: knowledge. They sell you that knowledge for a price. The price of the knowledge isn't a punishment. It's not that you didn't have the know-how beforehand to get where you wanted to go. No, it's a product and one that you must purchase in order to own it, to finally call yours after achieving your diploma.

Tuition isn't only a product that is paid for financially. It's paid in two other ways: time and effort. Consider this: a bachelor's degree requires you to invest four years of your time, on average. While you're paying in money, you're also paying in your time. While you're paying in time, you probably find yourself paying again in effort. Gary knew this thrice payment all too well!

It didn't take more than four days for Gary, a 2013 B.S./B.A. Marketing graduate from Bloomsburg

University, to recognize that some tuition is more expensive than others, especially in a new venture:

> *"The worst job I ever tried to do in school was the "bake sale" scheme. I say scheme because I don't know how anyone makes money from a bake sale where the items being sold aren't donated for free. Four of us made dozens and dozens of cupcakes and cookies. By the time the sale was over, we had lost about four days of our time and close to $30 apiece. It wasn't worth it, and I want my college friends to avoid the ruse of a bake sale."*

Ramen, pizza, and bakes sales aside, it's a good thing to laugh at the futile attempts for financial solvency. These are learning experiences that come from life and are attained through time and effort. You're paying for your tuition right now, just acknowledge it. Acknowledge that you're going after something bigger than yourself, and it's costing you. Yet, it's worth it.

QUESTIONS TO CAPITALIZE ON YOU:

- When was a time you remember that you had to 'put your time in?'

- Fill in the blank:

  If I never would have [insert your answer above], *I would have never experienced or known or met* _____ _____, and because I put my time in, I now know_____ and can _____.

- What do you think is the most expensive resource you have? Money, time, or effort? Why?

- How have you decided to 'pay' with your time, money, and effort? How do you know you've received value for it?

Chapter II

Reaches & Safeties:
One Way In, Multiple Ways Out

R eaches. Safeties. Did you hear those words a time or two when it was time to start thinking of college? I certainly did! And whether that's the norm or not, I simply don't know. However, in my life atmosphere, those words were daily utterances I heard from my high school sophomore year forward.

In my college preparatory high school, the pressure to perform was both top-down as well as, admittedly, self-driven. There wasn't a question of *whether* a girl would go to college or not. You see, I went to an all-girls school in which it was competitive to gain a seat in AP classes, where honors classes were a step down from the top, and regular, non-AP or non–honors courses were a mark of underachievement. The pressure was intense, especially for a naturally competitive perfectionist like me.

The stakes were high to do more than "well." Parents, for the most part, were actively involved. The teachers were well-degreed sticklers for precision whether in our chemistry notebooks or the punctuation on our Walt Whitman analysis essays, and the administration kept their eyes closely glued on us, given the tight-knit environment of an international day and boarding school.

While there may have been slightly more weight placed on academic achievement, we were encouraged to have some balance, the type of balance that pleases college admissions officers; one or more varsity sports, equestrian or art, positions in student government, participation in Key Club, etc. These were some of the ingredients in a recipe that would possibly result in admission to… a safety school. A safety? What about those reach schools? We wondered, collectively, if those applications would ever be good enough for a reach.

That's where the line blurs, isn't it? What is a safety, and what is a reach? Historically, a "safety school" was one that was thought to assure acceptance. The "reach school" usually was thought to have tougher standards, which they used to accept students; however, these criteria are blending because of current high school educational trends of AP and advanced classes. Many students leave high school with higher GPAs than were achieved in the past. The "four point scale" no longer applies because so many classes are weighted differently, and this weighting can differ from school system to school system, muddying the waters even more. Every student, every application, and every school is different, making the guarantee of any admission, safety or reach, a crapshoot at best.

Well, it's personal. Let me say it again: it's personal. Why? Because you are a person with a unique blend of knowledge and skills. That doesn't change. Regardless of the school you accept as yours, the track is usually the same as you continue through, trying out majors, applying for a myriad of internships, trying your hand at a few ventures, and taking that first job. Your knowledge and skills may change, but they are yours. They make up part of the person you are. You are not defined by whether you find yourself at your safety or one of your reach schools. One of the biggest shocks I had in my first weeks of college was discovering that each personality I met walked into my life the same way. Actually, we all walked into each other's lives the same way. We all applied, all were accepted, and all walked onto campus with a 'clean slate' as equals. For some, it was their safety, and for others, it was their reach.

Crafting our high school experience for that perfect recipe didn't diminish the fact that there was only one route in: the application. Once we were accepted, the playing field evened. The thought of safeties and reaches all combined. We had made the decision for the best school of the lot at which we were accepted. And we showed up for our education.

For some, showing up cost a bit less financially. Scholarships for athletes were far rarer than academic scholarships. To those hard-working few who obtained full-rides, athletically or academically, that was a feat worth commendation! For others, though, the financial aid formula was more complex and required an 'eye on the ball' motivation.

I'd venture your experience isn't so far from mine in that you also observed how others arrived on campus and how they were paying for it. Financing your education is just part of the business exchange we talked about in the previous chapter.

2013 Bloomsburg University graduate Gary explained his approach to financing his education this way:

> *"I knew that going to college and enduring the loan process was all worth it if I could get a good enough job. I didn't like taking out the loans, but my family was in the "middle zone." This is where you make just enough money to not get any student aid, but you make too little to be able to just write a check for the whole thing."*

And sometimes, after you've showed up and started your degree, the best of paid plans can change. Sometimes, there's a financial aid disruption, such as not qualifying for a subsequent semester or even a substantial tuition increase. Even the best laid plans can be disrupted, can't they? Jenny, a current Oklahoma State University student studying English and Psychology, understands that agility is required when the unexpected happens, like a tuition hike:

"I expected I would work at some point, but that I would never need more than a small part-time job to live comfortably. My financial report looked like I would have enough money to barely work; unfortunately, tuition rose so much that I was short several thousand dollars per year by the end of my junior year in college. I transferred for that reason... my senior year (I transferred and had to take a "super" senior year.). I often worked two jobs at the same time with 15+ credit hours and, yet, barely had enough money to keep myself going. There was not much money for entertainment or fun activities...medicine or vacations in that final year."

While it may have appeared after "Fresher's Week" that financing your education was set, it may not have continued that way. The playing field might have become 'unleveled,' and you're just unsure how to get back on the field. If you feel yourself scrambling even after you've finished your degree and are staring at your loan notices, listen up! Whatever financial path is chosen going in, paying for college in full each semester, obtaining loans to offset grants or accepting scholarships, the path going out can only be chosen by you. This is the path that will impact the rest of your life. And that path, whether in music therapy, software engineering, or whatever you have chosen, always reflects how you were created, not only what you know or can do. Who you believe you are is illuminated through your character. Your character is what your career will be built on, not vice versa.

So let's set aside for a moment that blueprint career plan that you'll follow out of college. May I ask you a couple of questions?

What sets you apart beyond that perfectly crafted college admissions application? What is it that you bring 'in' now that you're in college? I ask because you are the same person who walked onto the campus on day one. You are the same person who's put in your time and who's overcome obstacles and will continue to do so. You're the very one whose character will define the plan and blueprint of your life.

Time-travel back with me to meet a young man whose career blueprint left little room for adaptability, a young guy who would have been our Millennial contemporary in his time! His name is David. He's been popular across centuries and recently received accolades in the form of a 459-page book from one of the leading sociologists and thought leaders of our century, Malcolm Gladwell. In *"David and Goliath,"* Gladwell talks about David, an underdog, and how he won against a giant. While I'll leave you to read Gladwell's well thought-out manuscript, there's a theme in David's story that I'd like to pull out for our purpose. While one of David's career crescendos was indeed knocking down Goliath, there's more to the story of how he came to that battlefield and even more after he left it.

Let me set the stage if you're unfamiliar with David's story. David's father was successful, and the family

24

agricultural business carried with it the expectation of continuance, if you know what I mean. For David, that meant a pre-determined career path. Whoever said, "There's no short-cut to the top," must have been familiar with David's non-linear career path. He had to start at the bottom. The top of the family business, if I may take the liberty of supposing his thoughts, didn't quite look like the long nights spent alone 'in the elements' that he might have envisioned. He put his time in, and for David that meant time with the sheep and the wolves.

In modern classified postings, his title may read something like asset protection specialist, aka security guard. In his time, though, David was a shepherd. With that job description came high feral interaction, low human interaction. The assets were indeed his father's sheep, and he was tasked as protector from wild animals that attacked at night. Imagine a transient lifestyle without friends, near complete isolation from humanity for long periods of time, as well as dangerous conditions and weather variations. If we are all honest, that's the worst job imaginable. But it was expected of David; it was the one way into his career, to follow in the family business. His knowledge was passed down, families talk family business.

Well, David didn't just ideally sit by all those days in the fields, letting the sheep wander off and the wolves have their way. He showed up, he learned, and he paid his tuition in time. Also, the background story on David indicates that he brought himself into his work. What do I mean by that? He had a prescribed job with plenty of more experienced shepherds to offer advice and know-how. Yet it was he who learned how to play the lyre or harp, and he brought it with him to his job.

You see, he had a choice, just like you. He chose to put passivity or boredom aside and choose to deliberately look at his character. As he played and sang, he spent time thinking about Who created him and how he was created. He made his work, his job, personal. Just like you, he was a person with unique knowledge and skills. He needed an outlet within the confines of what was expected while doing what he had to do, learning through his experiences.

After the sheep were counted and after putting down the harp for the night, I wonder if David thought something like: *Could there be more? Something else? Something more fulfilling or something that was 'more him?'* Sound familiar?

Yes, David, there was more! His way out was paved by his uniqueness, but he just didn't know it. Yet. And there is a way for you as well, a way to move forward into the future you want debt-free.

Fast forward from those shepherd fields to David's crescendo moment, the one when he overcame a big challenge in a huge, public way. He was the same shepherd guy, wearing new armored clothing, when he met a commander of the army, a man who appeared defeated with no 'top warrior' to send forward to the front line and, dramatics aside, who knew annihilation was imminent. Then steps forward a young man energized by who he was and Whose he was. He was ready. In that pasture, he was alone with himself and his Creator. And he invested his time the best he knew how. He wrote page after page of prayers that were unread. With no audience, he did it anyway. He did it for himself and the One to whom he was faithful to, and during that time, he found new courage, courage to step into the role that a nation needed, a warrior.

So let's bring it back to you. When you don't have an audience, an admissions counselor with a list of dos and don'ts in a book in front of you, or a personal hero's blueprint of life steps etched in your mind, what are you doing? When no one is asking, watching, or listening, what are you doing? Like David, are you making use of your time to develop who you are and what you can uniquely do? Or, are you distracted by only what you see and the 'boredom?'

If you're still not convinced about David, let me tell you the next part of the story, complete with palaces and royalty. After David defeated Goliath, he didn't get a ticket straight to the 'high life.' Back to the fields he went, but not for long. The influential king of David's nation struggled with a big problem: anxiety. (If you've received the letter regarding the graduated or flat rate repayment schedules, you might understand anxiety that is deeper than a fleeting worry.) Opportunity is when a solution meets a need. Well, this was an opportunity for David to solve the king's need.

King Saul had the resources to find a cure for his ailment and desperation led him to ask his advisors for music therapy. He needed a musician to strum away the anxiety that his doctors couldn't alleviate. One of these advisors had heard about a shepherd who had a skill, and into the king's palace was summoned harp musician by day and warrior shepherd by night. It's a near oxymoron. And it changed the course of his life, but not immediately. You see, David couldn't help but play. Even if it was just to his sheep, he played. In the quiet, he improved and put in time, more time. Eventually, given the type of talent he was uniquely given, the sound of his skill went out beyond himself. Important people talked. They knew him for his dedication, his knowledge, and his skill. Those midnight hours of playing and prayer didn't go unnoticed.

The king offered him a salary and David entered his service. Yet he had responsibilities to his family business, to his father and to his flock. Splitting his time between harp-playing on salary for the king, a highly prestigious role that truly helped a man of influence, and shepherding, a role that helped his family, David built character. He lived every day well. If he hadn't been a devoted shepherd, he would have lost his flock. If he hadn't cultivated and practiced his song-writing and musical talents, he wouldn't have built a reputation of musical excellence. If he ignored his responsibilities and ran fleetingly toward the next thing, he wouldn't have been known as the courageous man he was becoming. Consistent with his growth, David became the next king. David, once a lowly shepherd, patiently waiting in the fields, making the best of his lot in life, became a king. He was given more responsibility and recognition.

A friend of mine calls these times that David made use of 'the waiting rooms of life.' That phrase begs me to ask this question, "What are you doing in the waiting room?" College, a string of interim jobs, and taking time off are all waiting rooms. Maybe you have a few other times that qualify as 'waiting rooms.' I had to answer this question more than once, and it always caused me to evaluate and then change what I was doing. Always. In essence, it caused me to invest more in character-building than attempting to force my situation to change, which, quite honestly, I tried to do more than once.

After I graduated business school and returned to the States to chart a career change, I recall having what I can only label as 'energized frustration.' The front desk at the exercise club knew me well, as the elliptical was my exertion of choice starting at 7 a.m. One morning in particular, I remember the hill intervals on the screen and a bitter mix of frustrated tears and perspiration traversing down my cheeks. I was aching from uncertainty about the next step to take in my life while every step on the machine felt familiar: hard. That morning, though, I'll never forget crying out in my mind, "God, please give me something, an acronym or something! I've been waiting so long. I'm tired." Without losing my rhythm, amazingly, I received exactly what I prayed for. No, my life didn't miraculously unfold, and my iPhone didn't ring with 'the answer.' I heard an acronym that has repeated itself so many times, in so many "waiting rooms," WAIT: *Willing Acceptance of Invested Time*. I certainly couldn't have come up with that myself, especially given the downtrodden state I was in. But it's true, so true.

As you're waiting, there's an opportunity to not just look toward something in the future, but an opportunity to take in the 'here and now.' You have the opportunity to invest yourself in what may, by all accounts and viewpoints, be a time of waiting. Like David, you can invest your time well and that leads me to ask, "What does your waiting room look like?" Maybe it's that course that wasn't on the schedule this semester, the one you need to graduate on time. Maybe it's an hourly job that looks like a dead-end.

College student Miranda's 'waiting room' was filled tourists. She worked at a local tourist attraction near her college:

"While working at a very popular tourist attraction, my friend and I would pass time thinking up new products that customers would want to buy featuring the store mascot. We also created a board game that was inspired by a combination of Monopoly and Life. The idea was to give the player insight as to what it was like working as the cashier and as a customer. We made cards that would add or take away points on a luck-draw system, like "Customer drops Icee in the middle of the store and blames the manager. Lose turn while you clean up the

mess," and "Cashier puts your money on the wrong gas pump. Go back two spaces while you wait in line again." We tried to build humor in it while showing both sides of the story."

She invested her time in that waiting room of another college job to make ends meet. Did you notice how she didn't just show up but invested herself and her ingenuity? Taking an active role in the waiting rooms of life is a choice. It will always lead to a different road out, each one marked by your character.

Wherever you are, whether on an elliptical or pushing paper or launching your next cash venture, invest well. Invest in developing your responsiveness, which will in turn develop your character. Remember, there may be only one way in, but there are multiple roads out. Take the high road!

QUESTIONS TO CAPITALIZE ON YOU:

- When was the last time you entered a 'level playing field' situation? How did you show up?

- Define character in five words. Does it sound like you? Ask others to do the same. Do they think their definition sounds like you?

- Next time you're in a 'waiting room,' whether in line, negotiating a price, or elsewhere, take a neutral check. What thoughts come to your mind? Frustration or intention? How about powerlessness or perseverance? Which thoughts do you need to get rid of to effectively invest your time in the 'waiting room' more beneficially?

CHAPTER III

ROADMAPS & BLUEPRINTS: THE JOURNEY TO SUCCESS LOOKS JUST LIKE YOU!

D o you remember every year around your birthday, standing up tall against that laundry room wall? Mom had tears in her eyes as she marked with a pen, your height and your name. A strange way to celebrate, isn't it?

Maybe it wasn't a wall that you remember or even your birthday. Just maybe it was standing in front of that short little tree in the front yard, maybe eye-rolling; the tree you stood in front of for a photo every August or September, the first day of school. After just a few years, though, that tree got taller as it gracefully aged. (Meanwhile, those school fashion trends didn't fair quite so well!) Those measuring tools, as nostalgic as they are, didn't tell you where you'd go. They were uniquely you. Your sister may have been on the same upward path of growth, but her pace was different. It just wasn't you!

That's the same as the blueprint for getting into college that we just discussed and also the 'roadmap to success.' What is a roadmap after all? I think it's best described as someone else's journey to the same destination you're after. It's a plan that can be imitated and, yet, will never look precisely like your journey.

As you grow up and start adventuring on your own exciting journey, remember that there's no one else's name on that journey but yours. No one has had the same set of experiences that you have had. No one has the precise skills and talents that you possess. No one has fought the exact same fear in the exact situation, which showed the courage you possess!

If you doubt you are courageous, stop right now. I challenge you to think back to the state championship, the submission of your last fiction piece, or the last thing you did that no one but you knew, or appreciated, just how hard it was to complete. That's some of the courage you're holding right now.

Those roadmaps and blueprints, read them for what they are: someone else's journey that yielded the results they wanted. Determining that your journey must look exactly the same doesn't leave room for the person you are, does it?

What can be gleaned from others are lessons learned, a term if you're in business school that you'll hear more often than not! "Lessons learned" are principles acquired by others who have gone before you, whether to college, in your intended career, or elsewhere. They are those things that you can listen to or read, and tuck into your memory for use on your journey.

Watch for your own lessons learned as well, which are often buried in the unexpected or even hardships. Take, for example, Miranda's experience as a student pursuing a B.A. in English and Creative Writing:

"My parents fell into that gray area of middle class that made too much money to qualify me for grants or certain loans yet not enough to afford the classes. I ended up working during the second semester of my first year to help pay for books and food, and it was just a part-time job at a fast food joint, which would not help me pave my foundation as an editor or writer. Thankfully, a little determination allowed me to excel, and I was promoted to management, which gave me invaluable leadership skills."

Miranda's journey took a turn like many college students. However, she had her 'why.' Miranda's 'why' was her willingness to take a seemingly off-the-path step in order to pursue her dream of becoming an editor. Had she stuck to the blueprint or the roadmap, she would have missed out on something she now sees as highly valuable, something uniquely part of her that she didn't even know until hardship knocked on her door: leadership. Side-steps often reveal another interest or aptitude.

The 'why' behind your endeavors provides the opportunity to experience 'more,' like King David, journey further in your uniqueness, and provides a compass even when the direction doesn't appear to be north!

This isn't your typical linear thinking, is it? In fact, it may run precisely counter to the advice you've heard for the past five years! Just as those pencil marks on the wall and the tree in the front yard are far away at your old family home, there's a new way to see how far you've gone and what's ahead on your journey. No, it isn't prescriptive or even a how to get from standing here, maybe in debt and the middle of your degree, to landing a noteworthy first job. But it does give perspective and replaces those blueprints and roadmaps.

I think it's time for a visual. In geometry, we are taught that a line always has points, and those points can be used as marks for measurement.

In music, we are taught that linear progression always has a passing note, a means to lengthen the melody in our ears.

In biology, we are taught that DNA is a twisting strand, resulting in our unique genetic code.

And if life's experiences are viewed in terms of points on a line, passing notes, and twists and turns, doesn't that leave room for a great deal of questioning? Without a known end point, how can the experiences be measured, and how can the goal be reached?

In my own journey, I viewed my degrees, work experiences, and businesses as points on a line. But I kept looking back at the past every time I reached a point of transition. Each and every single time, I became unsure of my decision and determined that I was again starting over with every point on my line. I didn't possibly know how they could all be leading in a straightforward direction. In short, I needed a new lens, a new visual.

Not seeing things right, I asked myself, "What if I stopped viewing my career and life in terms of stops and starts, points on a line? What could my journey look like instead?"

We are all inclined to a certain amount of reflection and introspection, but right now, let's challenge that way of thinking together. What if each experience or mile marker on your journey, such as that concerto honor or last day at your dream internship, looked like a circle instead of a line? What if all that education as well as those experiences and relationships were arrows on that circle and that circle actually a compass?

Let's get literal. Picture for a moment a certain timeframe, such as your freshman year. Dig back and create an ad-hoc list of things that stick out in your memory, perhaps move-in day, picking your first set of classes with your advisor (after waiting an hour for that over-achiever ahead of you to finagle those 21 credit hours perfectly), or perhaps even how it felt returning home for your first break and feeling the relief of stepping out and leaving to pursue your "why!"

I did the same exercise, and it hit me: life looks more like a circle or compass than a line. With my values, faith, and beliefs about myself fixed north, everything else was just an arrow on a circle. Can you visualize the trajectory of the arrows? Certainly! Each experience and piece of knowledge leads to the next, without losing momentum!

Whereas, that line with points perpetuates a certain unease while questioning if each experience, including when you found yourself needing to earn your way through school, was the 'right' or 'best' choice! If you know Who is north and what that means to you, the questioning quiets and is replaced with certainty in your journey, wherever it may lead.

Remember Miranda's journey to becoming an editor and the financial struggle she encountered? Well, she didn't just have that one fast food or trying-to-pay-the-bills experience on her journey:

"Unfortunately, I didn't always have the money to pay for a large enough course load to defer the payments...During these times, when the payments became due, I had to sacrifice study time to grab additional part-time jobs to both pay the loans and save up for the next semester's tuition–and hope I could afford enough classes to defer payments... again...I took many jobs that I didn't like and knew would have no impact on my résumé, but if I didn't pay the bills on time, I wouldn't be able to ask for more loans or qualify for larger amounts."

Without knowing her 'why,' and seeing each work experience as leading to the next, Miranda could have walked away from her dream. Every semester, she faced that conundrum of needing to take more steps on her journey toward her dream of becoming an editor and acknowledging the restrictions of her loans.

It's often when these barriers on the journey arise that you can precisely and without hesitation name yours, I'm sure, and that definitive choices emerge. Not the type of choice where you choose which of the two job options poses the lesser transportation headache or the highest pay with the best prospects of decent co-workers. No, it's the choice between believing that the barriers are bigger than your dream or putting on the lens of faith that the barrier will make your dream tangible, often in ways you could have never imagined or predicted. It's the choice between letting that slightest hint of fear that things won't work out for you manifest or encouraging your 'why' to supersede the circumstances at hand.

Your 'why' is just as unique as you are. And it takes the precise amount of faith that you have been given to move forward on your journey, whether it's to create the next technology giant from your dorm room or sit alongside hurting children while teaching art therapy! The barriers may have already appeared, and now is the time to remember what's on the other side.

If you remember reading *Pilgrim's Progress* in your high school literature class, you may also find yourself reading about a strikingly authentic main character aptly named, Ordinary. Like Pilgrim, Ordinary was on a journey inwardly and outwardly. There is a parallel parable-style book by Bruce Wilkinson called *The Dream Giver*.

The story starts when Ordinary finds himself living in his hometown of Familiar and was an Anybody, doing the same thing day in and day out. That is, until he woke up one day to a Big Dream! Uncertain about leaving Familiar, and with several Anybodies trying to talk him into staying, Ordinary contemplated what it meant to become a Dreamer. And here's the part of the story where the stakes are high and the choice clear, where the journey was uncertain but the 'why' undeniable:

> *"Ordinary saw his choice clearly now. He could either keep his comfort or his Dream...If his fear wasn't going to leave, he would have to go forward in spite of it...Ordinary shut his eyes and took a bold step forward – right through the invisible Wall of Fear...On the other side of that single step, the exact one Ordinary didn't think he could take, he found that he had broken through his Comfort Zone. Now the wall of Fear was behind him. He was free and his Dream was ahead. He began to whistle again as he walked on, his Big Dream beating in his chest." (25)*[xiv]

Like Ordinary, you've probably already come to a point when your 'why' has been questioned. If you're like me, you have had many times when you needed to keep that circle, the compass, at the forefront of your mind.

Take courage! Keep moving forward, resolute that one experience leads to the next, on your unique journey. It's *your* journey. Claim your 'why!'

Questions to Capitalize on You:

- [In ten words or less, fill in the blank] My 'why' for being in college is

  _____.

- As you seek out and receive advice professionally and personally, how do you filter what is useful or not for your journey?

- When you read 'unique you,' did you believe this to be true about you? Why or why not?

- Ordinary had to move past the 'Wall of Fear' and was surprised at what was on the other side! List the talents, skills, knowledge, or resources (including mentors or family or coaches) that can propel you forward on your journey.

- Who is one person you could reach out to today and ask for something you need to pursue your next goal?

CHAPTER IV

DREAMING ON: THE DIFFERENCE BETWEEN LIVING **IN** DEBT AND LIVING **WITH** DEBT

I t was 2007, and the word 'recession' was apparently something that happened back in the 80s, maybe around the time most of us were born. We certainly didn't know. All we knew was that the best was yet to come, and we were on the cusp of 'the best!'

We had all received the email some months before that our business school experience would kick off with a two-week initiation. Day one and all 115 of us, hailing from 40 countries, awkwardly found our seats in the brand new lecture hall of the Imperial College Business School. We had trekked from our far away hometowns to the South Kensington neighborhood, ready to 'get ahead' with a one-year intensive business management Master's program.

It was a new journey, and a faculty member took it upon himself to remind us first thing during orientation week to register our Oyster cards. As if we could forget, while finding flats in the crazed September London real estate market.

Opportunity cost. That was our introduction on that Monday morning at 9 o'clock with all our eyes assessing our soon-to-be-friends, soon-to-be-comrades, and soon-to-be-competitors in the job market during that thing we'd only heard of: recession!

Cueing the professor behind the podium, we were asked to get out our newly minted Imperial pens and A4 notebooks. Task one, day one of business school; this was our assignment: Write down everything you forwent in order to be there that day.

We must have given him a collective and striking blank stare because, tapping his marker, he said, "Think about what you left behind. You all left your families and moved on your own to a new country. You could have had jobs or job offers that you forwent. You are sacrificing a year of earning to pursue higher learning, aren't you? That's opportunity cost, the value of all possibilities forgone to pursue one chosen option: your Master's degree." Little did we know that the opportunity cost would reach even higher in the reports that came out after. Students graduating without student debt had seven times higher net worth than those students holding debt…and their degree.[xv]

But before the substantiation of our degrees and financial opportunity cost, something else clicked, at least for me. Opportunity cost went far beyond the financial that some had already paid or would pay in the future and tapped into an area I wasn't sure I wanted to acknowledge: the psychological commitment of leaving Familiar for Unknown, like Ordinary in *The Dream Giver*.

And consequently, sitting in that seat that now should have a plaque with my name on it given the number of hours I sat upon its padding, I came to understand that the cost of bringing a dream to fruition isn't paid in dollars, initially. The cost is first paid in your very imagination! And that's a resource that no one else possesses; the ability to take unique you and transform your dreams into reality. Your reality. A reality that others can then experience as a gift from unique you!

Right now, your reality may include an upcoming move on – or off – campus, an extra 3-credit language course to prepare for your study abroad, a leadership role in a political activism group, or even an application for a Fulbright. These dreams aren't 'free,' are they?

Until now, we've been looking back at the reality that money is money, aiming for where we're going by viewing education and experience as continuous, arrows along your circle encompassing unique you. We've looked at how character builds careers and that times of waiting are an invitation to invest time wisely. And now, we're looking at dreaming on, being all in, acknowledging the costs when they make themselves known, and capitalizing on you to move forward!

This very moment, your moving ahead requires effort. It requires the honest appraisal of how much time, energy, and capital is required to move toward your dreams. The question is not – 'Is it worth it?' – though it's part of the appraisal process. Rather, straight to the heart of your dream, I encourage you to ask yourself this: "How can I use the costs to propel me on? On toward my dreams?"

Your dreams will always precede cost, and by keeping your eye on the goal, it makes the costs visible and manageable. It's not a coincidence that the word order is 'opportunity cost.' First is 'opportunity,' followed by 'cost,' not vice versa. This is critical to how you assess the outcome of your education. Your time, your energy, and your capital are all resources at your disposal. You have the ability to exactly rein those in for your purposes and bring them under your management to propel your dream, and your life, forward. Even in debt? Yes. Even debt can be your motivation and not a necessary evil or even a burden.

A well-known speaker and entrepreneur was holding a seminar in his home on the subject of success principles. The event location was situated near the state university, and a student came up to him at the end of the talk.

"I'd really like to learn more, but I need some motivation. Are there some books you've read? What books can I read?" the student excitedly asked, taking full advantage of face time with the speaker.

"You want a book? It's called your checkbook! If it's in the red, that's your motivation," the speaker laughed.

If your checkbook or your student loan reminders came to mind just now, as you chuckled nervously, there's a reason. And there's a decision to be made on just how you will use your time and energy. Will you live *in* debt or will you live *with* debt, temporarily? A children's classic illustrates this in only the way kids at heart can understand!

Before the days of reading Socrates and Plato in Philosophy, there was another author whose characters you probably held before you could read: Alan Alexander Milne.

While Milne's name may not evoke the slightest memory, his friendly cohorts might: Winnie the Pooh, Tigger, Piglet, and the notoriously pessimistic, Eeyore. Do you remember that little donkey who could have everything right in his world, yet he would hang onto one thing or the possibility of one thing to paint the canvas of his day? Even when it was sunny, he'd be sure rain was coming! If Eeyore didn't keep us happy readers, relief came in his opposite-in-every-way co-character, Winnie the Pooh. He had a great attitude, didn't he?

While Pooh stared at the same sky as Eeyore, he was oblivious that the weather could change. He knew circumstances could change, but what was always on his mind? It was his goal: honey! When the clouds came, or a log fell on his path, it didn't become Pooh's focus, at least for too long. No, he kept listening to the rumbles in his tummy and went after his next pot of good, old honey!

And therein lies the parallel between living *in* debt and living *with* debt: Living *in* debt is the embodiment of the Eeyore complex, when you allow debt to paint the world grey at the first appearance of hardship. Without a life purpose, a dream, or rumbles in his tummy, Eeyore readily and easily gave up hope.

With a mindset of living *in* debt, you easily make choices that are reactive to what's seen, that temporary 'makes ends meet' position appears to be the only option and will never develop into anything remotely useful professionally or financially. When you're faced with new opportunities, but living in the mindset of being *in* debt, those loans could be the very thing that hinder you from launching into future you imagined.

Conversely, a mindset of living *with* debt delegates that right position of debt in your future, a so-called 'means to an end.' Debt simply isn't part of you but can be a catalyst you can *leverage* in finance terms or *manage* in business terms! You have the ability to use your student loan debt to your advantage, no matter how you feel it's affecting your options and opportunities. Your debt is temporary. Something that you are not while living here on earth.

Consider your smartphone. When you picked it out, you bought the hardware, which came preloaded with certain functions like texting, an alarm, photo storage, etc. Also likely pre-programmed was the fantastic app called either the App Store or Android Marketplace. Tap that app, and a whole new world opens! If you're like me, you've probably downloaded an app, excited by the functionality and the clever way it could help you, and then actively used it the next few days. Then, whether it's that running app that helped you train for your first half marathon, or the ab-move a day for your six-pack, you realized you weren't using it as much. You just don't need it anymore for one reason or another. The marathon is complete, or you have your six- pack abs. So what did you do? You deleted it, and with the tap on the 'x,' it was off your screen.

The debt you have is no different than that app. You went into college debt; you used the capital for a time and a purpose, and now you're working to pay it down. Then, one day in the not so distant future, you'll not need the debt because it is paid off completely. You used it and now don't need it anymore. In essence, it's not in your hardware. Your debt is yours, but you are not your debt. You may be living *with* debt temporarily, but you don't have to live *in* debt mentally.

Remember Gary who tried his hand at the bake sale scheme and can laugh now about the time and money he lost? He's pursuing his dreams *with* his debt, recognizing how to use it to move forward:

> *"I respect my loans, but I don't let them dictate my life too much...[the loans] definitely affected the type of work I looked for. It didn't necessarily dictate what field I worked in. I already had decided...and [the debt's] affect was on the minimum salary I needed to search for, and it also gave me a timeline..."*

Believe it! You have the ability to capitalize on yourself, paying off your debt at the same time as pursing your dreams. Isn't it time to start thinking beyond the

Eeyore complex and with hope for your future, knowing that debt is your temporary catalyst?

With your skills and abilities in hand, you are able to overcome debt with the hope and confidence given to you long before you were even born. As a man named Erwin McManus so aptly says, "Humans were designed to create futures." You were created to create a future for you, and you weren't left without those resources: your unique skills and ever-growing knowledge. But there are two more resources, and these two aren't temporarily used for your disposal, like the app on your phone or the loans you took out. Rather, hope and confidence, when combined with talent and skill, always point ahead toward your future. All of these – skill, knowledge, hope, and confidence – combine to beckon you to steps in faith. And the very circumstances that challenge your faith on the journey, often appear to stand in complete opposition to you, and this is when hope and confidence propel you past the barriers and on to your future.

Filmmaker, TED speaker, clothing designer, author, community activist and international speaker, Erwin McManus, certainly understands the tension of a journey. He's quite transparent, in fact, about his struggles and pursuit of what he should 'do' or 'be' and all of the barriers he faced in uncovering what to do and who to be. With a wide range of advisors and influencers in his life, McManus had more than a little time to understand what dreaming is and what it means for the future, his, yours, and mine.

Critical to the fruition of any dream and the creation of a future, he says, are both confidence and hope:

"Confidence is usually built on what we know and where we've been. Hope is built on what we don't know and where we haven't been. When you hope for something, it's in the future. When you've prepared for something, it's in the past. Thrown into the future, you're a citizen of the future, no longer a prisoner of the past."

So what is it you're holding onto? Now is the time to embrace where you haven't been, what you haven't done, and move forward with hope and confidence.

You've been preparing and will continue to prepare much of your life. This time of study, or recently finishing your studies, has prepared you. Only you know what it is you are hoping for because only you can see it. Only you are dreaming the dreams for your future. And the only way those around you will ever see the realization of the dreams, now with debt, and soon without, is for you to hold on to hope. Continue in confidence and dream on! You are worth it.

Questions to Capitalize on You:

- Whose outlook on circumstances and goals mirrors your own most closely, Eeyore or Pooh?

- What does making choices out of hope and confidence mean as you look toward your next job?

- Does it seem like there could be other opportunities to pay off your debt other than a traditional hourly job?

Chapter V

Hard Work or...Hardly Working?

Sophomore year, I had my eyes set on living off campus and getting my first apartment. As much as I enjoyed the ready-made friendships of dorm life, I was ready to step out, decorate my own place, and establish my independence.

Then, my parents threw a wrench in the plan. While they would pay for my dorm and board, they wouldn't pay my expensive upper Northwest DC rent. So much for independence, I thought! All I saw were two options: live another year on campus in a cramped room or in an expansive one bedroom near the embassies! Little did I know I had that a bit backwards. Undeterred, I knew there had to be a way. And so, while in Prague, I faxed back the rental agreement to my Korean roommate to submit for our shared one-bedroom apartment right on Massachusetts Ave. #211 was soon to be ours, complete with that classic rattan chair and IKEA dresser I thought was the height of interior design at the time.

Committed to the 12-month lease, it was time for me to get financially creative. I knew that minimum wage simply wouldn't make a dent. So, my criteria for a job looked something like this: above minimum wage, cash, and the possibility of studying and writing my papers during work hours. Too good to be true? I didn't think so, though I knew my list could be a little stretch.

I decided to nanny for a newborn. With a few nieces and nephews 'under my belt,' I thought a newborn would provide the opportunity to earn cash while being able to work on my hefty workload of 18-credit hours. I decided I wanted to graduate a semester early as well as pick up a minor. I now laugh at how easily my plan could have backfired with one little condition called 'colic.' I would have sunk faster than the Titanic! Fortunately, I came into a wonderful family who 'adopted' me, and I was able to make my rent as well as eat more than ramen! (That was another condition of my employment; I needed to make enough to support my grocery shopping at Whole Foods!)

Babysitting is certainly not a new idea for making money in college! But it represented the beginning of a shift in thinking. Perhaps, even right now, you're in the situation I was; you need a good income to support your two habits of eating and living indoors, while studying. My purpose of following my dream away from home to a global city and pursuing studies in international relations and public communications was so I could get the job I was after. "That job" would certainly morph over time because of the shift in my thinking that happened while nannying, while working hourly.

In hindsight, I was on the cusp of something: Moving beyond the hourly mindset to making my own money. I just didn't know it and couldn't even describe what was shifting. Here's what I did know: It was really difficult to maintain a good attitude knowing I needed to stay at work to make a few more dollars. Why? Because the whole reason I needed money was to study until I graduated. Honestly, it is not an easy thing to balance studies and work. At some point I recognized that my priority, my study time, lessened the more hours I put in. (The newborn didn't stay inactive, and soon it was playtime at the park with my laptop left at home!) In other words, hourly was hourly, and I didn't have enough of those hours to work and study.

Balancing earning and studies certainly wasn't only my isolated experience. And if you're like me, you may be able to relate to Haley, a student at Texas A&M University, who dreamed of working with children. She needed an education to transition from her dream to her reality. And so, she found herself in the midst of her degree with a growing passion and expenses growing even faster. So, what did she do? Here's how Haley tells it:

"I looked everywhere for work. I probably applied to 200 places, looking for a traditional type of job. Some [of the jobs and businesses] that my friends and I came up with in college have been all over the place. I have done

everything from babysitting to dog walking. I have sold some unused possessions [online] and at yard sales. I have been paid for taking notes for other people's college classes because I know how much some people hate going to class. I have taken temporary positions such as being a secretary or filling in for a busser at a restaurant. I have also worked as a freelancer [creating] logos, [writing] articles, and [proofreading] papers among countless odd jobs."

A shift was occurring in Haley's thinking as well when she took on the note-taking job, asking herself, "What is something that is already part of my life or something that I'm already doing that I can turn into a money maker?" Or, put another way, "How can I not have to input more time to get an increase of the output of cash?

Input and output is that precious function of time and moving beyond hourly earning. It means that you have to prioritize two things, one of which we've already discussed: your dream. The other is your time. Unique to every human on earth, whether billionaire or salary-earner, is that we all receive only 24 hours to invest in our day. How you invest is up to you, not just in the waiting room of life, but in each and every single day. Until you recognize time for the scarce resource it is, the only-what-is-seen mindset will exclude you from the myriad of opportunities that you can take hold of around you.

Moving beyond the hourly mindset isn't an escape from responsibility at all. It just offers a lens through which we can see opportunity. But before we start opportunity spotting, let's take a candid look at what working hard means and its antithesis, hardly working.

If you're cringing, there's a reason. As the proverb says, "As water reflects the face, so one's life reflects the heart."[xvi] When we acknowledge that what we produce is a reflection of who we are, who you are, work becomes increasingly meaningful. For that which you produce is a reflection of not only how you view yourself but also how you value work. Take a look at why you'd say one friend is a hard worker and the other isn't. They are communicating through what they do or don't do, how they value themselves.

However, if you place your personal and financial value in only what you produce, you'll feel you are worthy when you're doing well in your classes, your side job or business is booming, or you received public recognition from your internship boss. Enjoy these times, but know *your* value isn't based on what you earn. How much you see direct deposited may just reflect how you view earning.

When it seems as though your work isn't getting you the results you expected, a high mark on the final, a sales bonus, or landing a large contract with a local business owner, be wary of assigning your value to those results and output. For if we do, if we buy into a results-oriented mindset, we turn into our harshest critic whose opinion shifts with circumstances. Where then is that hope and confidence?

It's counter-cultural to abandon the control of outcomes and embrace the hard work of working hard, isn't it? Don't throw away your goals so quickly and become locked in a here and now. This is the fertile ground where hard work and your dreams collide, the time where you bring your mind's eye dreams into the present by developing yourself, your value of your limited resource of time, and how you use it. Just watch and see what opportunities present themselves and the new solutions you discover when you hold on to working hard, not to gratify those watching, but for yourself! Others will see, and as the saying goes, "What do you do when no one is watching?"

Now, you may be asking, "But where do I start? I understand that I need to 'dig in,' but I also don't want to get 'locked into' what I'm doing now." And the simple answer is, in effort. If hard work is a car that will get you from the 'here and now' to your dreams, effort is the gasoline to keep you going. Without it, that car will stay in the exact same place in the garage, just like your dreams won't become your reality.

If there's one character trait of the Millennial generation, it's that we don't enjoy remaining 'parked' for too long. It may be in your nature to continually pursue your 'what next,' to ask questions, to determine the best way to move forward. A recent experience underlined this dynamic so exactly of the tension of working hard and figuring out how to draw best on time and effort that I have to share the story with you.

The folding tables were arranged in a rectangle to encourage discussion, and after finding our spots, we each took our turn introducing ourselves. It wasn't a spectacular or out-of-the-ordinary way to begin a meeting, just a normal start to people meeting each other for the first time. And we were, after all, business professionals by day and writers by night. The bookshelves all around us of the attendee's publishing ventures proved the point.

We all took our turns and about three quarters the way around the table, it was his turn, the guy in the corner. I looked over and something just registered as something not looking right. Nothing in his appearance stood out, but there was just *something*. I didn't know what it was at first, but then it settled. While we were all surrounded by bookcases and the antique smell, to boot, I noticed that right behind him, as the next attendee to introduce himself, were a few paintings. An unusually high visual person, I admit, I momentarily 'checked out' to take in the three lovely landscapes, each watercolor-quality of architectural renderings, and the fourth. That fourth one was a mono-color abstract of three female forms quite different from the other three. A bit peculiar, but I turned my focus back to the next person, thinking at least I figured out what was strange!

He hung his head, staring at the table as soon as the group's leader nodded his turn.

"I can't decide if I'm an artist or a writer," he mumbled. No, "Hi, my name is _____ and I do _____." I literally chuckled out loud at his authenticity, but I quickly quieted it into a nervous cough because, awkwardly, I noticed I was the only one amused! "That's my stuff, behind me," he cocked his head. And it made sense. Over his left shoulder were the hardcover books he'd published and over his right, the four paintings. His effort was evident, and his hard work absolutely undeniable. How many published authors do you know who are able to translate their thoughts not only in words but also in oils and watercolors, in landscapes and abstracts?

One thing was visibly obvious, he didn't spend much time considering where to start. I doubt he labored long over which to become, or when he should start one or the other. No, it was clear that he put his time into what was right in front of him, pen and keyboard or brushes. Then, he went to work. Had he never put in the effort, let alone displayed it for others, those of us at that table certainly would have never seen what was in his mind's eye. And I never would have received his lesson: what effort results in (while asking copious questions doesn't produce a thing).

I forgot to mention this: he was in his early 70s, nowhere near a Millennial but still trying to figure out what 'to be!' Yet he had a commonality with us and the life experience to relay this: we aren't one thing, one title, one job, or one business. We can be many things, if we make the decision to embrace the many titles we hold, the interests we possess, the dreams that we imagine, and the journey marked only with your name, my name.

But releasing the outcomes, as well as the need to be one thing or go after that one thing, seems counter-intuitive, doesn't it? You choose one major to the exclusion of every other degree offered, yet there is no guarantee a position will be available in that field. You can intentionally study and earn the degree, yet you have to split your time between a combination of jobs and studying to earn your way through. It's times like these that you realize the journey to get into your career and out of debt is harder than anyone told you it would be. It may seem you are working toward your dream, and yet reality seems to be working against you, financially at least.

The wisdom lies in recognizing that you don't need to be all things. Pick one thing now, recognizing that it will require the full investment of your time and effort. And in that one thing, what would it look like if you removed the 'hourly' component, if you ventured or determined to start or do something that didn't have a clock-in or login? What if you could take your time and combine it with effort right now to produce something bigger than your time limits? That's something to go after, especially when overcoming that temporary necessity of repaying your loan debt.

Thanks to the popular ABC television show, Shark Tank, you don't need to head over to the business school on campus and enroll in a dual-degree to 'dig in.' Make your 'one thing' into your *something* with some pointers from America's favorite Sharks.

After watching a few episodes, you'll come to realize that Kevin O'Leary structures his deals either on licensing or perpetuity. Why? Who doesn't like residual income? Meanwhile, Barbara is a product gal who likes to foster relationships with her entrepreneurs to help them grow in sync professionally and personally. Meanwhile, Mark Cuban makes his initial decision based on personality. Cocky owners are shot down, unenthusiastic owners are passed by quietly, and those high energy, agile entrepreneurs, they are the ones who capture Mark's attention and, consequently, his wallet.

While each one of the Sharks represents a different investment personality, the range of advice offered to entrepreneurs is worth tuning in to watch. Think about it. You can gain a business course by investing one hour a week! You'll notice the common thread: those entrepreneurs who are only half-invested in their heart, their wallet, and their time commitment simply get passed by. Why? Because the intangibles, such as confidence, hope, hard work, and effort combined with skills and knowledge are the ingredients for success no matter the 'thing' or venture. Recognizing unique you always precedes the creation of unique ventures. Just like the entrepreneurs, and the Sharks in the tank, whatever work or venture in which you invest yourself reflects how you value yourself and that precious resource of time.

So what does it take to obtain your dream, working in the interim, balancing it all, and putting in the effort? Whatever it takes. Take it from Bonnie, who you'll remember eats more than ramen, a student who's been there, done that, and worked hard:

> *"My goal was to not have student loans, which is exactly why I'm doing whatever I can to save up money. I believe that this definitely had an impact on what jobs I was/am willing to do. I wasn't too picky because I knew that I needed to make money, and little projects can add up to big balances. Also, one time projects...help grow your brand, thus acquiring more work through referrals or the same clients you've worked with in the past!"*

Capitalizing on you to move forward requires whatever it takes. And it takes you, working hard and showing those around you your effort!

QUESTIONS TO CAPITALIZE ON YOU:

- Which individuals in your life display the character trait of working hard…and hardly working? Whose mindset does yours most closely mirror?

- Have you been trying to be 'all things?' What are a few of the 'many things' you'd like to pursue? Narrowing it to one, how much time and effort today is required of you to move that dream forward?

- In order for your 'one thing' to come to fruition, what do you need to forgo and commit to for that dream to become a reality?

- [Fill in the blank]

  Today, I'm making a commitment to do _____ every [pick a time frame], _____ so that I can achieve this goal. I'm going to tell [the name of a trusted mentor or advisor]_____, so we can celebrate my success when I achieve it!

  Signed, [Your name]_____.

Chapter VI

Listen Up & Listen In:
Spotting Opportunities Inside
and Outside Your Field

With my piping hot coffee in one hand, and my other hand pulling my slightly oversized carry-on, I made my way to the coveted legroom seat. Feeling 'set' with not only my pre-departure coffee but also my only-while-traveling-do-I-sit-down-to-read-this magazine, I was truly looking forward to 2.5 hours of rumbling relaxation.

But my row-mate didn't quite share my same plan. As soon as I was situated, she began asking me friendly questions, which I later learned had an ulterior motive of the romantic sort, for her son! Staving off that initial annoyance, which I sincerely hope I'm not alone in admitting, I settled in for what I realized would be a long, long flight.

And it was during that interruption that I listened to a story that actually was an inspiration, of sorts, for our conversation, this very book! So, why did I wait until the last chapter to share it? Listen in to our conversation:

"So you're in school? That's so nice! What school? Oh, you know, I have two boys, and they were in school. Well, they were until a few years ago. They both graduated and oh! Let me show you a picture of them. Isn't he handsome? And here's the other one, but he's married. They are just so smart. Did I tell you what they do? Well, actually, they didn't plan on doing it. But it just kind of started while they were in college, and I just have to tell you the story. They're just so successful and doing so well financially..."

Notice that there wasn't much of a dialogue? That's because it was literally a monologue, and I'm so glad it was. The words you speak are indeed the lessons you keep. Here's the story she shared about listening, and the very thing that offered you and me the opportunity to have an authentic conversation about your dreams and your unique self. Humor me in that this could be you with the ability to move from living *with* debt to moving onward!

The two sons had a pretty common shared interest for guys and gals: cars. Out of necessity, to get to and from the campus of their Midwestern state university, they needed a set of wheels between them. But they didn't want just any cheap 'typical' college car, whatever that meant to them.

They wanted a Mustang. A Mustang would get them some attention, they decided!

So that clunker they were sharing, they decided to park it at the end of the short driveway of their frat house. And they put a sign in it with a hefty mark-up. The dream Mustang was, of course, an upgrade with an upgraded price tag that they couldn't afford. The clunker sold quickly due to a steady stream of potential buyers thanks to the frat parties. It sold so quickly that prospective buyers didn't know, and their phones kept ringing for test drives. But the car was gone.

Cash in hand, but still not enough for the Mustang, it hit the brothers: why not get a couple cheap cars from their earnings, put a marked up price tag in the window, and flip them? After all, what college student has ever successfully bought a used car from a dealer on a student budget? Here was their thinking: Our customers would be our classmates and friends, and they could just come to us with cash and leave with a car.

So it began. "A college student used car lot in the back of a frat house lawn," their mom, my 2.5 hour row-mate, proudly gushed. Naturally, I was curious about what they did now, but I didn't have to ask.

"They are just so successful, and their dad and I can't believe it. They're just your age!" (After I was able to convince her that I was indeed a bit older than the initial teenage assessment!) "And you know, they got their degrees, and you wouldn't believe it. Well, we can hardly believe it, but maybe you can since you all are so alike.

They own their own dealership, a large Ford dealership with a big, brand new building. And they are just doing so well and drive whatever they want now! You know, they are just doing so well," she beamed proudly.

And I sat there wondering if those two had ever imagined they'd now talk cars every day and have their pick of the lot, literally! Mustang in mind, they did what they had to do initially to improve their transportation to get to and from classes. Whether knowingly or unknowingly, they listened up when their friends started talking. I'd imagine those conversations were far from formal and probably pizza and beer-laden. But they listened, and, as a result, spotted the opportunity. Why? Because they first had the ears to hear, then the eyes to see.

Perhaps you've been there – the place in time when you've decided it's time for those dreams to come to fruition. Or maybe you just can't make that next loan payment, and the pressure is like none you've felt before, and it's time for a big change. Both are forms of desperation, aren't they? The first is an eager and accelerated hunt to achieve, to have, to receive that which you've been working so hard for, right now and not later. And the latter is a search for a quick escape, solution, or balm to end the pain of financial hardship. And desperation, in isolation, can lead any of us to do things we wouldn't under normal circumstances!

That's when, what I call a 'pro-bono' board of advisors, comes in. A few years out from my degrees, I found myself in this seemingly cemented-to-my-circumstances position that was a lethal mix of wanting to accelerate my dreams and de-escalate the tension and anxiety of my own debt. I was grasping in desperation and going after so many things that my head was spinning. And nothing helped to relieve the pressure.

Part of my daily routine was to wake up at 5:50 a.m., go to the Starbucks below my condo, and center myself for the day by reading and writing for an hour. It was on my way to ordering that I noticed the same people every day, and in particular, a table of a few retired and middle-aged men and one woman. After a series of exchanged smiles, and then the exchange of names, I was offered a seat at the table one day. It was probably the most worthwhile invitation I've ever received. Here's why: this group had a wealth of experience in starting, buying, and selling businesses and companies that didn't read like textbook pages. They allowed me to sit in on their thought-processes and emotions in the choices and transitions of their ventures.

I received the most beneficial gift of my career: friendship. As they casually and perhaps unknowingly poured their knowledge and wisdom into me, they also listened to me. They listened to my ideas, and in a quiet way, tempered them and me with encouragement and words of experience. It was not a mentoring relationship, per se. There is always a risk of draining your mentor. Learning the balance of asking for their time and using it well is something learned with time. Yet, joining in an existing conversation beside seasoned professionals was personally highly beneficial.

Developing a group of individuals to whom you can listen may open an opportunity for you to share and to be listened to, to share your opportunity spotting because listening always precedes seeing. A lens of faith always requires taking off a lens of fear. And it's always more blessed to give than receive. Give your ear first to those around you, whether your classmates, like the now car dealership owners, or the experience resting within your pro-bono board of advisors. It will always result in a new lens for you to see the opportunities, the very ones that you're after.

You see, others are also on their journey, and there are individuals who have encountered similar obstacles as yours. While you are certainly venturing on a journey as unique as you are, wouldn't it make the walk more enjoyable if you could "bounce off" others along the way? To give and also receive that attitude of gratitude? There are individuals willing to walk alongside you. Are you willing to walk alongside them as well, listening in and listening up? After opening your ears and then your eyes, don't be surprised if you find your dreams accelerating, your debt diminishing with your hard work, and, yes, more opportunities in plain sight!

QUESTIONS TO CAPITALIZE ON YOU:

- Who do you already know in your life who readily shares his or her experience?

- How would you define a good listener? Does it sound like you?

- If it's time to move beyond hourly, capitalize on you and take that opportunity. What's stopping you?

Chapter VII

Opportunity's a Knocking: 25 Springboard Ideas

U niquely you, the opportunities you see won't be visible to everyone. Your unique skills, gifts, and talents, and the lens through which you open yourself to seeing possibility, is not duplicable. Who you are and what you value will carry you through your journey and into as many dreams as you imagine making into reality. And that reality may be just as obvious as needing to sell your car or making money tweeting at a wedding. Are you curious about how those two things could ever pay down your debt? I'm glad you are!

In this final section, you'll find 25 opportunities to give you a launching point for your new mindset. One of them might just resonate. My hope is that these ideas provide a springboard to get you thinking creatively. You have what it takes to launch a low-capital venture utilizing the talents and skills that make you excited! Each opportunity isn't necessarily a formula (because we throw those out along with the roadmaps and blueprints) but is a launching point for you to get started now on that venture you've spotted! Here's how each section is organized:

IDEA

The idea is just that, an idea that is characterized as being quick to start, cash generating, and requires little to no capital to begin.

GETTING STARTED

This section takes a look at the initial steps to go to market, from idea or inception to landing your first customer.

THE NITTY GRITTY OF PRICING AND OVERHEAD

The sole goal of starting a venture is to substantiate it with profit…fast! This section offers insight on pricing and just how much cost or overhead will be deducted from all that profit you'll be bringing in soon! After all, the bottom-line is…your bottom-line!

So here's to moving forward, capitalizing on you!

1. Think Pop-up!

THE IDEA

Foodie markets, outdoor art fairs, indoor sports equipment shows, Indie concert weekends. What do all these have in common? They are temporary, one-time events in a designated location. There's an organizer, vendors, and customers. That's it. Now, let me ask you a question: Would you like to be the customer paying an entrance fee and money for souvenirs? Or would you rather be a vendor, purchasing the space or opportunity to showcase skills and also selling products or performing? While you can indeed make some money possibly on the vendor end, think about walking around for a moment. Who do you think is collecting the money from the vendors and in all likelihood *not* sitting under a tent, at a table, or stressing about cash at the end of the pop-up day? It's the organizer, the mastermind behind the event!

GETTING STARTED

Consider what you know and who. Are there a lot of foodies in your network of college friends? How about crafty gals with a penchant for design? Take a look in your local community, in newspapers, class offerings, etc. Find out what's hot, and if there's a certain group of business owners that could use more exposure. They are your clients, your vendors!

THE NITTY-GRITTY OF PRICING AND OVERHEAD

Like any venture, there is some risk! Think about the location for the pop-up; an area with high visibility and potential for foot traffic is ideal. Or perhaps a hotel ballroom would be more conducive to your customers' taste. Rank your top three locations, pick a date at least four months out, and call for pricing. Consider offering sponsorship opportunities to offset the costs of the initial space reservation. Then, sell, sell, sell the spaces to your vendors! Bring in a social media expert, get a QR code, print some business cards through Vistaprint (www.vistaprint.com), send out press releases through a distribution site, such as PRWeb (www.prweb.com), and knock on vendor doors. Don't forget that Facebook page as well, which allows you to solicit and promote vendors as well as build excitement for attendees.

2. Foodies: Bottle, Bag and Box!

THE IDEA

Remember Grandma's famous fudge, chock full of those antioxidants (chocolate) and all-natural ingredients (*real* sugar instead of those substitutes)? Or how about Aunt Susan's homemade Ranch dressing with that twist she told you and no one else last 4th of July? Laugh if you will, but many an entrepreneur has taken what they know and bottled, bagged, and boxed their way to a business. So, why not you?

GETTING STARTED

In the United States, food laws are overseen by local and state governments. Many states have a thing called "cottage laws," which are pro-small business owner and outline the profits that can be created from home-based businesses, food, and more. For example, in Florida, a foodie can produce and sell out of his/her own home or farmer's market up to $15,000 in goods, given correct labeling and a few other state-specific requirements. These laws vary extensively, so doing your homework is important! Trusty Google is the place to start. Try a search on "Cottage law" and "(your state)." You might be happily surprised to find out that your state enables you wide distribution, possibly even online.

THE NITTY-GRITTY OF PRICING AND OVERHEAD

Economies of scale in the foodie business are key to your profitability, so know your recipe! If you're dealing in fresh produce, consider finding a dealer at your local food terminal or farm to negotiate a flat rate and delivery day. Packaging sells product, whether you're getting into a Whole Foods test market or selling online. A good place to expand your packaging knowledge, access a community of foodie knowledge, and get the kitchen space you need is YourProKitchen (www.yourprokitchen.com). This franchise is popping up in new markets like hotcakes (excuse the pun) and offers foodies not only the opportunity to glean best practices from one another but also rent kitchen time complete with professional grade equipment on an as-needed basis. No more galley kitchens in city apartments or unsanitary dorm kitchens! Once you've determined your raw material and production costs, test similar homemade products and see how your margin would look if priced similarly. Start asking others who are in the business about profit margins, pitfalls, and best practices to help you succeed!

3. Tweet It Up:
Wedding Social Media Concierge

THE IDEA

Imagine that friend's wedding you couldn't go to in Italy but would have loved to have seen the glamour of the day? Well, it's possible, isn't it? Those days of guests holding up their Otterbox-laden iPhones and snapping a pic of the first kiss, have been monetized! And now you can be that paid guest to document all the moments through live Twitter, Facebook, and Instagram posts for the happy couple! The W Hotel Group (www.starwoodhotels.com/whotels) is the first to offer a Wedding Social Media Concierge, and the charge is steep at $3,000. But what if you catered to the mid-market under your own brand?

GETTING STARTED

The wedding vendor business is a tight-knit group with a vested interest in each other's success…and referrals. Check out your local chapter of the National Association of Wedding Professionals (www.nawp.com) or find your area's wedding planners through the American Association of Certified Wedding Planners (www.aacwp.com). Reach out to these wedding planners, florists, cake decorators, and more, highlighting how your social media will help expand their reputation and work.

(After all, who doesn't like looking at beautiful cakes on Instagram, mentally noting the design, and even the decorator for the next special event?) See these professionals as your spokespeople and do the same for them. It's part of being in a community, isn't it? In other words, *be the referral you want to receive*!

THE NITTY-GRITTY OF PRICING AND OVERHEAD

Wedding social media concierge services is new to market, meaning you'll need to feel your way through pricing like every entrepreneur who's first to market. When you receive quizzical looks, capitalize on the fun. This service isn't necessary, but it's a way to connect those out of town guests who can't make it. It's a way to document the festivities, and it's a way to create fun memories on your timeline. Ultimately, it's an add-on in an industry lush with wants, not needs! To get your foot in the door, consider approaching the special events and meeting coordinators at area hotels and reception venues. See if they'd be open to listing you on their options packages! They would mark up your services to grow their bottom-line as well to be on the cutting-edge of a new trend! An additional bonus: given that most events take place on weekends, your school work won't suffer!

4. All Those Swipes Cost Money: Credit Card Processing

THE IDEA

That meaningful piece of plastic, a credit card, is over six decades old but still holds the same purchasing power as when it was first introduced by Diner's Club and then American Express. And the consumers holding the card are just part of the transaction, transferring your money to a restaurant, store, or company for that must-have. The credit card processing industry continues to grow because as more and more entrepreneurs pop-up (like you!), they need to accept payment and not just cash. So, they need a credit card processing company that not only gives them the equipment (the terminals or phone swipe for mobile businesses) but also links Visa, MasterCard, Amex, Discover, and Diner's Club to their bank account! That's called merchant services. These credit card processing companies need a sales force on the ground to sell business owners the equipment and access...and that's where you can come into this fierce cost-cutting market!

GETTING STARTED

First Data (www.firstdata.com), North American Bankcard (www.nabancard.com), and Flagship Merchant Services (www.flagshipmerchantservices.com/) are a few of the dozens of merchant service companies that offer competitive splits to the sales force or affiliates. One of the key benefits is a residual income, meaning that you will earn on all the sales that the business owners swipe, once you get them set up. It takes some education, though, and a great mentor who knows the ins and outs of ethical sales. Competition to get a merchant to process through your company is fierce, and customer service will sell you every day! Start reading and googling 'Merchant Services Affiliate Program' to educate yourself on the processing industry. Registering with one of these merchant service companies will require online training as well as a background check. But don't be deterred and keep networking with local business owners.

THE NITTY-GRITTY OF PRICING AND OVERHEAD

When a customer checks out at a storefront with a credit or debit card, there is a fee associated with the swipe. It's a service provided by the merchant service processor to transfer funds and assume the risk between the business owner and the credit card company. As an affiliate, you will receive a split (sometimes 60/40, 70/30 or other) for every time a swipe is processed. The fee and split is comprised of a set swipe fee and usually a percentage of the sale. Through training, you'll learn all about pricing yourself so as not to gouge the business owner and to monetize the hard-earned contract with the business owner! As you explore and sign up with a processor, you'll likely have access to your own business cards, local leads, and other marketing materials to position yourself as both knowledgeable and trustworthy to your potential clients!

5. The Brokering Appeal of Used Cars!

THE IDEA

If you're not in a big city, having transportation in the form of a car is a luxury, isn't it? Or maybe it's a downright necessity! If it's a necessity for you, it probably is for your friends as well. Take a look around. What are they driving? Is there a market for connecting the cars to their anxious new owners…for a fee?

GETTING STARTED

You know your market and the types of cars driven. Maybe you're in an American-strong area in Michigan or near the Honda plant in Alabama or Ohio. Focus on a brand or price point you are financially comfortable with and fairly certain the market demands. Explore the local car auction sites and potentially team up with a veteran who can get you in. Reach out to your college business professor or even approach a local car dealer (making sure that you're not competing in the same price-point market!). Explore a partnership. Then, take the plunge and buy a car to flip. You might even want to take a look at Swap-A-Lease (www.swapalease.com) to do a buy-out locally for resale. And always invest in CarFax (www.carfax.com) to shore up the deal on both your end and the resale!

THE NITTY-GRITTY OF PRICING AND OVERHEAD

Pore over Kelly Blue Book values (www.kbb.com) to establish values in your niche market and make sure you can readily 'spit out' prices when asked. Focus on your first car acquisition and the timeline in which you want to flip it. Reinvest in the next purchase. It will require some upfront capital but only as much as you have access to!

6. Focus First:
Special Events Videography

THE IDEA

Thanks to the iPhone, amateur videographers (and photographers) are plentiful. But when an organization, non-profit, association, or the like is hosting a special event, this type of footage just doesn't cut it! Organizations are increasingly turning to promotional as well as informational videos to connect with their stakeholders as well as potential clients, customers, or donors. Whether displayed on a YouTube channel, posted to the homepage through Vimeo, or even sent through email, video communication is on the rise, and special events are a prime location to cash in on your skill. If you enjoy videography but not the editing, why not form a partnership with a design pro buddy in Adobe Premiere or other editing software?

GETTING STARTED

A common concern when starting any venture is to honestly address the start-up capital requirements. To brand yourself as a special events videographer, you'll need access to equipment, if you don't already have it. Consider testing out your communication department's rental cache by volunteering to cover an alumni event or something similar. The benefit in doing a no-cost gig at your university is that you'll not only start your portfolio, but you can narrow your dream equipment. Then, head online to find what you need, new or used. Now, you're set to start your market research and begin selling!

THE NITTY-GRITTY OF PRICING AND OVERHEAD

Asking first is key to determining the market need, isn't it? In the case of special events, pick a few medium-size organizations (those who will have the liquid resources but probably don't employ anyone full-time with video skills). Take a look at their website and see if they currently use video as a medium and note when they have their next event. Preparation is everything! Then, through their website or LinkedIn (www.linkedin.com), find the communications person, potentially someone with the title of Director of Communications, Community Relations Manager, Donor Relations Coordinator or similar, and give him or her a call. Talk about scenarios where you can interview the event guests discreetly and the value of documenting success, if the event is a fundraiser or awards evening. Ultimately, you want to underline the value that your skill and product (video) will bring to the company. Remember, you're selling an add-on that might not be in the event budget. But that objection can be overcome by discussing the value and benefits!

7. Localized Touring with a Flair

THE IDEA

Button-down sweater, fanny pack, and long umbrella? Those may have been the tour guides of the past! But suffice to say, you probably don't have a single one of those in your wardrobe, for a reason! Let's move out of the yesteryear of tour guides and into 'localized touring,' an opportunity to guide interested individuals into a corner of the world that interests you.

GETTING STARTED

Make an appraisal of your local area and the obvious 'draws.' If you're in my hometown area of Northeastern Ohio, one 'draw' is the Niagara Wine Valley and the production of ice wine, a type of wine produced from grapes picked after the first night of frost, creating a sweet, sugary red wine. Tours of the vineyards already exist, so why reinvent the wheel? However, what is a parallel to wine? Cheese. And it just so happens there is a growing underground cheese culture! So, think about the uniqueness of your area. Are there a few delightful chocolate makers? Or how about a plethora of ethnic restaurants? Maybe there's an opportunity to tap each restaurant's specialty course. Think about planning a trolley tour, stopping at one restaurant per course with demonstrations at each. Or perhaps there are a number of abandoned buildings in the area. Could you, legally, create an urban exploration-themed tour? Time of year may also play a factor as well as weather, and by creating a package of three, four, or more tours, you can rotate them throughout the year! Forgo a website at first and go the social media route with bookings by phone. Photos sell experiences and that's your product: a memorable experience!

THE NITTY-GRITTY OF PRICING AND OVERHEAD

Two words: Parents' Weekend. How profitable would it be to join with the student union for publicity to do your launch tours during Parents' Weekend? Whether you live in a tourist area or not, cater to locals at your launching. After all, your customers may have even visited a stop or two on the tour, but they are after an experience! And that's the heart of your venture: to provide conversational 'bragging rights,' so your customers have something to share that's 'in the know' at their next party. And you know what that means? Great Experiences=Enthusiastic Customers=Word-of-Mouth Publicity. As your pricing, see if you can't get negotiated fixed rates with your 'stops' on the tour. Highlight to the vendors or business owners that they'll benefit from exposure and customers delivered right to their doorstep! Create an exclusive partnership with a trolley or limo company and offer mutual free advertising and kudos on your collateral and social media! Give first and get!

8. There's Always a Private Party Somewhere: Wait Staff Recruiting

THE IDEA

If long hours on your feet, spilled drinks, and shabby tips are nightmares that have crept into your reality, read on! Behind some of the hardest, most gross, and downright dirtiest jobs are managers who have often 'put their time in.' After learning the job, they've become overseers to ensure that the hard, gross, and dirty jobs not only get done but are completed with quality (hopefully!). And sometimes all it takes to shift from worker to manager is a change of scenery, from restaurant to hotel or private home. From waiter to waiter recruiter!

GETTING STARTED

Weekends are filled with private parties, anniversary celebrations, 90th birthday parties, children's birthdays, engagement parties, and weddings. Festivities are rarely complete without food, are they? A team needs to serve the food the private chef so masterfully creates. Meanwhile, the hostess needs peace of mind that she can enjoy her guests without the worry of empty glasses and the appetizers going unpassed. A wait staff team gives that peace of mind, but only if they are reliable, on-time, and polished. That's in short supply, which means there's a market opportunity. Rather than spending money on direct advertising, alliances are the key to moving this business from opportunity to repeat clients. On a private chef association website such as the United States Personal Chef Association (www.uspca.com) or the American Personal & Private Chef Institute & Association (www.personalchef.com), shortlist the private chefs in your area and reach out with your services.

THE NITTY-GRITTY OF PRICING AND OVERHEAD

Getting your foot in the door in wait staff recruiting literally means getting your foot in the door of the event location. Offer to do a small event with one or two wait staff and a personal chef. Contact a few of the most reliable friends you have who are seeking some side work on weekends or evenings. Let them know that you're testing the market with the intention of having ongoing weekly bookings. Early loyalty and mutually beneficial relationships with your freelance staff is key! Develop guidelines of conduct that will be used for interviewing/training your wait staff as well as a proof of concept for your customers. Set a flat rate per waiter, per hour, not forgetting preparation and clean-up time. Consider the split between you and your wait staff: 70/30 or 80/20. Remember, your time is valuable in developing the business that translates into contracted events, and their time is valuable as providing the service you are selling. In presenting your flat hourly rate per waiter, don't forget to mention that tips are welcomed and divided evenly among the staff of the evening! Do some research as well into local event planners who can also be a referral source both ways!

9. Direct Sales E-Writing: Scooping Up Those Communications Majors!

THE IDEA

You know all that spam you receive advertising lemon trees and the latest loan consolidation offer? What about those postcards arriving every day in your parents' mailbox back home for pool cleaners, plumbers, and pet walkers? All of those pieces of direct mail and sales emails were written by someone somewhere behind a screen just like the one you're carrying around. Why not put all that communications coursework in writing press releases and advertorial content to commercial use *now*, not after college?

GETTING STARTED

There's always more than one route into a new venture and writing a business' way to more sales is no different! Once again, take a look at who you already know and start asking questions to uncover the needs of those business owners in your sphere. Are they already doing email marketing, or do you get a blank stare when you mention Constant Contact (www.constantcontact.com) or SalesForce (www.salesforce.com)? The right questions uncover the pain of 'warm' contacts. Now is always the time to continue brushing up on your verbal powers of persuasion. Eager and hungry business owners will likely prefer the Dan Kennedy style of copywriting (Check out the Glazer-Kennedy Insider's Circle site at www.gkic.com), and you'll always want to keep in mind Dale Carnegie's principles in his bestseller, *How to Win Friends and Influence People*. Also, start creating a Word document 'swipe file' by copying and pasting phases and sales verbiage that works and 'hooks.' This file will be your go-to once you're in the midst of sales writing. Not to mention, it will save you a great deal of time without sacrificing creativity!

The Nitty-Gritty of Pricing and Overhead

Once you land your first client, you'll need to establish your credibility by setting a reasonable price for your services. You may find the business owner would like to create a 5-email series to send to potential customers who have registered on their website. Or they may be seeking a direct mail, postage-marked letter series to targeted pre-clients they've yet to meet, a 'cold' campaign. As you're just starting, you may not know how much time you'll need, so you'll have to estimate, perhaps an hour per letter, plus or minus. Then, set your hourly rate by taking a look on freelance sites such as Elance (www.elance.com). The LinkedIn Groups are another resource for rate and knowledge sharing (https://www.elance.com/groups/directory), where you'll find some groups specific to sales and copywriting as well as other skills. Remember, the business owner will certainly thank you for a flat-rate because just as you want to know you profit for your time investment, they want to know their exact costs!

10. Concierge Lessons: Home-Based Lessons Aren't Just For Music

THE IDEA

If you ever took piano lessons, chances are you might remember getting up on Saturdays, buckling into the car, and heading to that 'sit up straight' teacher's house for your piano lessons. If you thought it was tough getting up on your one day to sleep in, imagine how Mom, Dad, Grandma or Grandpa felt. It wasn't exactly convenient to take you to those music lessons that maybe you had begged for, but the novelty wore off pretty quickly. Or perhaps it wasn't music you were in to, but you needed to learn how to swim before that first year of sleep-away camp. The routine was the same. You had a full day at school and then had to hop in the car and go to the community or club pool for another hour before rushing home for dinner and homework. It wasn't efficient time-wise for your caretakers, or you, looking back, was it? What if you could create a venture around a skill of yours and take it on-site to busy people, including parents?

GETTING STARTED

You don't need to look far to see if one of your skills might be the right fit for on-location concierge lessons. Are you a certified swim-instructor? Why not offer weekly lessons, one-on-one, for local parents with pools at home? Imagine the value you'd bring to parents wanting their little ones to learn water safety and the convenience of not having to arrange for and drive to group lessons. (Check out Sunsational Swim School for inspiration: www.sunsationalswimschool.com). If you've done summer volunteer work in an English as a Second Language environment or even have your own certificate, consider taking your skills and either by yourself or gathering other instructors, go to local business owners with a predominantly non-English speaking workforce. Pitch your weekly on-site class services as a means to improving management communication. Or consider a youth audience, those little ones who are growing up in a non-English home but will soon be attending a predominantly English school for pre-school or kindergarten. Consider organizing and posting flyers for a fun, interactive weekly class to 'jump start your child for pre-school!' You have a host of other skills that others would benefit from and could learn from without having to go far from home!

THE NITTY-GRITTY OF PRICING AND OVERHEAD

Since you'll be going on-site and teaching one-on-one, you have the flexibility to charge more than traditional lessons. But remember, your clients aren't necessarily paying for your commute time, so plan your schedule carefully so lessons are in the near geographic area to cut travel and 'down' time. If you're teaching in a corporate on-site setting, have early budget conversations with the company decision-maker and price accordingly. If you can demonstrate long-term value and profit generation for the company, you're in a much stronger negotiating position.

11. Brew Mastering: Create Your College Blend

THE IDEA

Enjoying a cold beer doesn't always require a red cup! And before you turn up your nose at the mention of wine, have you noticed the increase in locally brewed beers and their followers? Similar to wine aficionados, the art and science of home brewing has beer drinking enthusiasts trading in their red cups for customized labels and brown bottles in bulk! Maybe there is a market in your area for a brewed-by-the-student-connoisseurs of a university mascot laden brew recipe.

GETTING STARTED

Whereas the store-bought stuff requires little more effort than popping a top, brewing your own takes a bit more knowledge, preparation, and experimentation. You don't need to look beyond online to source your two main ingredients for your brew: hops and malt. The other two, water and yeast, shouldn't be hard to find. Once you have those, do a bit more research on the four-step process and enlist a few friends as well. A few good starting point resources are "The How-to Home Brew Beer" magazine (www.byo.com/newbrew) and "The American

Homebrewer's Association"
(www.homebrewersassociation.org/lets-
brew/beginner/start-brewing/). The dorm kitchen
probably isn't ideal, so take a look into other kitchen
options like the one listed in *Foodies: Bottle, Bag, and Box!*
While patience is a virtue, and you'll have to wait a few
weeks for fermentation to make your brew delicious, it will
be worth the wait…and don't forget to write everything
down. Replication and consistency is critical to making a
name and flavor for yourself…and your university!

THE NITTY-GRITTY OF PRICING AND OVERHEAD

Since there's a bit more that goes into launching your
own beer brand, and scaling is a future goal, you'll need to
price yourself according to the custom, local brew market.
And remember, your customers may not be college
students on a budget, but rather the locals who come to
games. Your customers will pay for flavor and school spirit.
If you note a great deal of interest in the process and
sourcing of the ingredients, it just might make sense for
your wallet to offer some themed classes. The more you
learn, the more you can be paid to share!

12. Winning With Non-Profits: Grant Writing

THE IDEA

Generating profit revenue for a non-profit isn't an oxymoron...if you know how non-profits work! Annual galas, fundraising drives, mega donors, subscription campaigns. These are all sources of revenue that non-profits mix in order to carry out their missions. But there's another source that takes quick fingers and a penchant for sales, and that's grant writing. Researching grant-funding bodies such as private foundations and governments programs takes time and human capital, which in many non-profits comes at a premium! However, the research time spent solidifies the 'fit' between the investor or grant-maker and the non-profit. The 'sale,' though, comes in the actual grant proposal where dreams are clearly communicated! In order to win the 'fit,' precise use of funds and commitment all must be demonstrated, so passion is key!

GETTING STARTED

Freelance grant writing is something that must come from a heart to serve! So, think about causes that are important to you. Do you have a pull toward survivors of human trafficking and their safe housing that costs money?

Or maybe you've experienced the role of a sports mentor in your life and believe every child should have the opportunity to play, grow, and excel! Start asking around on campus, and also your professors who are locals, to develop your list of non-profits. Then, craft a one-page sales proposal. (For some direction, take a look at Patrick O'Riley's, *The One Page Proposal*.) Research the organization, list a few grant-making body matches to their mission, then demonstrate your skills through your track record in persuasive writing. While you might not have direct grant writing experience, remember sales and persuasion is fundamental. Also, get some pointers from the seasoned professionals at The Chronicle of Philanthropy (philanthropy.com). The non-profit may even have previous successful grants that you can learn from and model new ones after! Your sales proposal is your marketing piece and will demonstrate the quality you can deliver. Want to expand your horizons? Consider being a remote grant writer, following the same process of discovery and pitching!

THE NITTY-GRITTY OF PRICING AND OVERHEAD

Most grant writers are paid hourly and not success-based due to ethics. But developing a track record of 'wins' will allow you to increase your rate so always write with excellence! Take a look at the Chronicle of Philanthropy to gain a better idea of the going rates for professional grant writers. While you may need to start at a relatively low rate ($15/hr or more), that's not forever (see Chapter 2)! Keep writing, improving, and pitching larger budget organizations!

13. Tournament Champion: The Organizer Takes Home The Bounty

THE IDEA

The local pub quiz night is always a draw, and, rest assured, it's not just for fun…it's a significant moneymaker! The owners benefit from publicity, the lengthened time the patron spends in the establishment that night, and drink and foods sales. And it's a good time for showing off, kicking back, dueling egos, and walking away with the bounty if you play it right! Why not organize your own Tournament of Champions within a specific knowledge area? Maybe you're a gamer and well-acquainted with the week-end long tournaments or are a chess aficionado having competed on a traveling team. If you're neither, no problem! What is it that you and your friends do know a bit about and can create a fun, tournament atmosphere around? What about the techies? Could there be a time limited challenge to create the best website for the top-rated college eatery in the area or a new app for a campus scavenger hunt?

GETTING STARTED

As always, start with what you know and who the people you know *know*! Whether you choose the

tournament route or contest route, nail down a list of
sponsors to provide the advertising budget as well as
prizes. Give yourself a lead-time of eight weeks to book a
(sponsored) location for a tournament and leverage social
media to get the word out. Make it easy to get paid for the
entrance fee with a simple payment/registration on a basic
website (One option you can look into is OnePagerApp:
www.onepagerapp.com). If you're looking to run a contest,
such as an app builder one, brainstorm with your university
or a business client on the specifications to put forward to
participants. You'll ensure success for the client and make
sponsors happy by aligning expectations from the start!

THE NITTY-GRITTY OF PRICING AND OVERHEAD

Driving profitability for the event or contest comes with
multiple creative streams, including the entrance or participant
fee, sponsorship fees, and concessions if on-site. Know your
audience and consider opening the contest or tournament to
community participants as well. The broadened market could
increase your number of participants. When approaching
sponsors, ask them what type of exposure they'd like and
prepare at least three different levels of offering, including a
combination of social media and print advertising as well as
email blasts and day-of endorsements. You know that
participant email list populated by participants? It's worth
something! Offer it as a value-add for sponsors post-event or
price it into your package offerings. What company or
business wouldn't appreciate the opportunity to capitalize on
student email marketing for future services or products?

14. Taking the Fun to Kids and Making the Parents Happy: Mobile Sports Camps

THE IDEA

With the headlines reading of childhood obesity, and the youth diabetes rate near-epidemic, parents are looking for ways to get their children active, fast! Summer is the perfect time to get those kids away from the television and Xbox and to introduce them to the fun in the great outdoors through a sports camp! Elementary aged students are prime candidates for half-day or day-long camps, making it easier for working parents to minimize the summer childcare they need and to get their kids moving…toward fun!

GETTING STARTED

First, you'll need to take an inventory of what 'sports fun' means to you! If you're on a scholarship or play intramurals in a sport, why not offer a sport-specific week of camp, such as soccer camp? Now, you may say, "Don't those already exist?" They sure do, but you're not the one collecting the money and having a good time teaching little Beckhams! Maybe you're more the type that enjoys all sorts of sports and has a mind for creating obstacle courses and water games. Whatever the fun you like to have, re-create it with kids in mind so you enjoy it with them! Enthusiasm sells, especially when parents see that you're just as happy at the end of the day (though maybe with a hoarse voice!) as when they dropped their kids off with you that morning! Next, you'll need to identify a location. Inquire with a local Parks & Recreation board or even your own school or university! Negotiate a lower space rental lease with a multi-week booking. And don't forget to obtain the non-liability forms from the park or school, along with creating your own. If you hire others, pay extra for an online background check that you can then tell parents all workers have passed. HireRight (www.hireright.com) and PeopleStart (www.peoplesmart.com) are two resources to look into. Send out flyers to local schools as well as painting studios, tutoring companies, and any business that serves parents and their kids!

THE NITTY-GRITTY OF PRICING AND OVERHEAD

Your basic costs will include a rental fee for outdoor/indoor facilities, equipment (balls, cones, jump ropes, etc.) and those all-important snacks! You may need to hire an extra set of hands (and legs) if your group is beyond five children. Consider paying your employee(s) an hourly rate double minimum wage or a flat rate for the week. Even better, offer them a referral bonus for any children who sign up for camp through their word-of-mouth! This is how you grow a camp into a profitable venture! Also, if you recruit a stellar team of employees with those 'Wow!' sports credentials, tell your parents! The economics of scale is vital, and remember, you can easily design your daily programs to adapt to the number of campers. Camp should be a weekly rate with a drop-in friend option. Research competitors and their pricing, such as gymnastics camps at the local gym and hockey camps at the arena.

15. Faux Painting for Doctor's Offices

THE IDEA

Pediatric dental offices are popping up everywhere! And they aren't like your or your parents' dental visits! Young, marketing-savvy pediatric dentists (and pediatricians as well) are creating kid-friendly atmospheres in their offices, complete with interactive video screens in the waiting room, aromatherapy to calm those fears, and, yes, themed mural art adorning the walls to capture the 'adventure' of dental visits!

GETTING STARTED

A simple search of pediatric dentists, also called pedodontists, as well as pediatricians and orthodontists is a great place to start! Manta (www.manta.com) is a registry of small businesses that invites business owners to 'claim' their profile. Think Facebook meets Google meets Angie's List! The benefit in searching on Manta is that you'll secure the personal email address of the doctor or business owner, meaning you can go straight to the decision-maker! Craft a letter of introduction yourself or hire a freelance writer on Elance (www.elance.com). Include some pictures of your work, as well as, since that's what your selling, visual attraction! Then, start sending those emails. Why not also print some copies and go straight to the office to introduce yourself? Note: A Fine Arts background isn't required! Find some simple designs that cater to kids, i.e. geometric shapes, floral designs, whimsical scenes, or even emoticons! The easier the murals to replicate, the easier to teach others, meaning you could move into a management role securing contracts for your painters and muralists!

THE NITTY-GRITTY OF PRICING AND OVERHEAD

Your three key costs are your time, paint, and transportation. Be generous on how you value your hours but be sure not to quote hourly. This deliverable requires a flat rate, and remember, you'll also be working evenings and weekends when there aren't any patients in the office. Work-in-progress may not be desirable to your clients, especially if you're painting a highly visible area. Be sure to state a finish date and ask upon completion if you can display your cards for parents. Who knows? You could start doing residential commissions for the parents who see your work!

16. NAME-BRAND EBAY FLIPPING: DEVELOPING A FOCUSED PRODUCT LINE

THE IDEA

Many a casual flipper on eBay (www.ebay.com) has made hundreds and thousands of dollars in the fine skill of re-selling. And just as many have fizzled out, breaking even with the fees and not understanding the key! And just what is that key? (Google 'eBay selling strategy,' and you'll read some best practices.) Like anything else, success on eBay requires developing a niche, and in this case that means a focused product line. Think about your grandfather's train collection. While I'm not suggesting you run to box his sets and sell him on selling, I am pointing out that he knows all about the brands, can tell you why his are unique, and where he sourced them. That's because he didn't focus on every single thing manufactured in the United States in the first part of the century! He knew what he enjoyed and concentrated his time learning on a niche. The top eBay sellers do the same, whether it's Kate Spade authentic handbags, vintage Cartier women's watches, or Louis Vuitton luggage.

GETTING STARTED

Once again, what do you enjoy researching and learning about? What resources do you have at your disposal in the form of access to product (Goodwill stores, junk shops, garage sales, secondary markets), and who do you know (collectors looking to liquidate on commission, hoarders, storage unit owners)? Take a look on Amazon for some e-books about eBay best practices. Learn from others! Then, start acquiring! Once you sell a bit, you can request for eBay to lift your 10-item and $500 in listings per month. (That's called a 'seller restriction.')

THE NITTY-GRITTY OF PRICING AND OVERHEAD

Think about offering your services to non-techie collectors, maybe elderly individuals who aren't tech savvy but would like to empty their closets and garages. Think about also speaking to realtors as they have a client list of movers, both buyers and sellers, who usually purge before the big moving day! Working on commission is how you can get paid for your techie skills, such as taking mobile phone pictures, uploading them, and writing eye-catching listings! Or work on a fixed retainer in which you research product values, list them, and ship products all in return for a success commission percentage. Consider a 20% commission. You know how to value your retainer hours best. Log all your work to understand your default hourly and adjust your percentage. If you'd like to source your own product and not be an intermediary, you'll want to make sure your sale price is above the cost because those fees can add up! Do market tests to see what's hot and then start listing as quickly as possible. You'll realize that your buyers are a select group. Encourage them to message with questions and always direct them to another piece of inventory in your response. You might even become an exclusive product source with a small client list!

17. BRAND AMBASSADOR PROGRAM DEVELOPER: WHO IS NOT ON CAMPUS BUT SHOULD BE?

THE IDEA

Back before Redbull was, well, everywhere, it launched a massive campaign on college campuses across the United States. Who better to sell energy to than sleep-deprived students working on tight due dates and a week a semester of test after test? Redbull's success is undeniable and countless other brands have capitalized on the same market…you! For every student's car covered in a bright, bold branded decal, there are dozens of other companies looking to make an entrance onto your campus and probably a few more just don't know how to get more student customers, including some of those pop-up businesses!

GETTING STARTED

Those friends of yours who are bottling, bagging, or boxing their goods…why not start asking questions to see if their ideal customer base is right there on campus? Could other area campuses also benefit from the product, and what would happen to sales if you could land an exclusive contract with the campus stores or dining services? Keep your eyes open to the places you frequent. Perhaps even the local yoga studio would like to draw students in on a special. As a campus rep, you could negotiate an exclusive contract with the studio in which they provide you with a discount number. Print some cards and get to marketing. For every student membership, you earn money. Alternatively, consider working with another local medium-size business owner that would benefit from a 'best practices in campus marketing' strategy. As their eyes and ears on campus, you can take your knowledge and become their mouthpiece by tracking down advertising in the campus papers, sponsoring events, and representing at events.

THE NITTY-GRITTY OF PRICING AND OVERHEAD

The value of your repping is directly linked to the sales conversions the business or company receives. In other words, you need to demonstrate your knowledge of the college market, and the Millennial mindset for buying, by backing up your words with numbers. Initially, use other case studies until you've successfully worked alongside other campus start-ups or local businesses. You may need to pitch yourself as hourly in the beginning with a commission. But after a few success stories (and be sure to determine how you'll quantify success for each client *before* the pitch and contract), consider working on retainer, presented alongside a customized written strategy. If you can demonstrate how you've added to other companies' bottom-lines through sales on campus, you'll have a good foundation to negotiate a significant marketing contract.

18. Cake Smashing Your Way: Children's Birthday Party Photography

THE IDEA

If you follow any bakeries or cupcake shops on social media, you can't help but notice the popularity of those adorable one-year-old birthday boys and girls smashing their 10 fingers into a gorgeous cake! And just who's capturing that once in a lifetime moment? Usually Mom or Dad. But they can only capture the little one and not the delightful expressions of themselves celebrating with their birthday boy or girl! How often are parents playing host and hostess, caterer, photographer, and wearing a myriad of other hats during a birthday party they just want to enjoy? That's where you come in and offer your services as a children's birthday party photographer!

GETTING STARTED

Now, if you don't like kids and getting messy, or have no interest in capturing memories, read no further. But if you think photographing kids' birthday parties sounds a lot better than babysitting, bath times, and nighttime tears, this is the venture for you! First, you'll need to determine where your target parents are hanging out. See if there's a local Mommy and Me (www.mommyandme.com) class. Some other venues may include Gymboree (www.gymboreeclasses.com) or The Little Gym (www.thelittlegym.com). For those new moms with children who may be approaching a year old, see what exercise groups meet and who their director or franchisee is. A few groups to look into are Fit4Mom (www.fit4mom.com) and BabyBootCamp (www.babybootcamp.com). Another avenue would be to contact birthday party venues and offer your services as an add-on, giving the venue a percentage of your earnings, of course, in the contract!

THE NITTY-GRITTY OF PRICING AND OVERHEAD

You'll have to judge your market a bit for pricing, and this is where market research comes in. Talk with the venues as well as any moms you know, perhaps even any moms your friends are babysitting for. Consider a flat rate, a 1-hour or 2-hour appearance at the party. Note any shots the parent is sure to want, including posed family pictures. Guarantee a set number of proofs (50, 100, 150) with full editing. Offer all prints on a digital file for a set price, if you choose, understanding that will take away any opportunities to profit from printing upcharges. If you retain the rights to all your work (recommended), negotiate a print rate with a local printer and be sure to mark up all prints!

19. Trading Pics for Profit: Selling Your Study Abroad Pictures

THE IDEA

Thanks to our trusty phones, great quality pictures are just a click away! Now, if you're the next Ansel Adams, you still probably turn your nose up at the mere thought of photography and mobile phones being synonymous! However you classify your photographic skills, there's probably at least one luck shot in your mix that you consider to be reproducible. Instead of leaving it as your fabulous background, why not turn that study abroad shot of the Mayan artisans or the Hong Kong New Years' Skyline into some income?

GETTING STARTED

The quandary of every artist, photographer, videographer, and painter alike is putting a price on their creation. There are many routes to profitability! One such company that accepts contributions is iStock (www.iStock.com). But it's not as easy as uploading and earning, that is until you are a bona fide iStock contributor. To get started, you'll need to register your account, then after reading a company manual, you'll be asked to take a quiz on what you learned. If you pass, you'll need to submit

119

three samples for review, and then you are all set! The benefit of using iStock as, essentially, your distributor, is that you aren't limited to photography. If you are a creator of audio, a videographer, or an illustrator, you can also contribute your work. Bear in mind that you'll have to take that quick test in each of the disciplines you'd like to contribute to. Another option to explore is Dreamstime (www.dreamstime.com), which allows for non-exclusive contributors (meaning you can sell the same photo on multiple stock sites), exclusive images (those photographs you sell only on Dreamstime), and Exclusive contributors (meaning you're a loyalist and sell only on Dreamstime). The company also runs 'On Assignment' contests as well as featuring a referral program. If you have a blog showcasing your creative work, add the badge, and when one of your site visitors purchases stock on Dreamstime via your site, you earn!

THE NITTY-GRITTY OF PRICING AND OVERHEAD

Selling your visual and audio work is a royalty business, which means you can keep earning while doing the work of capturing those pictures or creating the illustration just once. On iStock, you're guaranteed 15% royalties for all of your images that are downloaded. If a customer is on a subscription with iStock, you'll receive a flat-rate royalty. Be sure to look into the requirements for becoming an Exclusive contributor because then your royalties increase to 45%! Selling your work on Dreamstime, you can expect to earn a 25-50% revenue

share as a contributor, increasing to a 60% royalty as an
Exclusive contributor!

20. What's Easy For You Isn't Easy For Everyone: Wordpress For The Small Business

THE IDEA

Web communication isn't yet part of every business's marketing plan, as difficult as that is to imagine in today's day and age! Business owners in recent years have seen the proof that social media and Google ranking can indeed help their exposure, but that doesn't mean they personally have the knowledge to execute even a blog. Remember that high school blog you created in WordPress? Well, there are small businesses that could use you and that knowledge!

GETTING STARTED

Sure, there are a host of full-service marketing firms and web design companies across the country. The larger the firm or agency, however, the greater the overhead, which translates into higher client consulting fees. Not all business owners prefer to work with account managers or can justify the expenditure. After all, no one knows the value of a dollar more than someone who writes his or her own paycheck!

THE NITTY-GRITTY OF PRICING AND OVERHEAD

Pending the complexity of your client's business, you may be able to get away with free service. But if they have registered a url, they will need that first, right? As an alternative stream of income, sign up as an affiliate with a web hosting company. Both Go Daddy (www.godaddy.com/affiliates/affiliate-program.aspx) and Bluehost (https://www.bluehost.com/cgi/partner) have programs that reward you for referrals. Next, factor in your client meetings as well as time to develop or hire out the content and design. Even if you have neither skill, you can still certainly be a creative director and sales person, outsourcing the actual deliverables. But you need to have some know-how, and it will likely be better for your developer to be local to build trust (and the potential for referrals) with your first, second, and third clients.

21. Creating A Solo-Entrepreneur Client List: Social Media Strategist

THE IDEA

Just for a minute, think about those people you know who really just work for themselves and don't have more than one other person helping them out. Maybe it's the personal trainer you see every day during your post-class workout. Or perhaps it's the physical therapist to whom your mom was recommended, following the accident. Or perhaps it's your family friend who left a large corporate law practice to narrow his services to his book of business. They likely don't have a great deal of time to take away from their income generating hours to boost marketing in the way of social media. Could you help?

GETTING STARTED

If you're looking to find clients who could benefit from increasing their presence online, it's going to take a bit more digging than going online. Think old-school marketing, such as flyers, newspapers, and local radio. Take a look at a local radio station's business listings or partners page. By looking here, you'll know that your targets do indeed see value in marketing (making it a conversion sale) and have a budget for it. Also, look in the services listing in your newspaper, specifically for the business card-sized ads. Consider your network, such as the people in your family's life. Now that you have a list of targets, it's time for you to start marketing. More and more, companies are also seeing the value of a LinkedIn corporate profile. But as you know, the corporate profile is also linked to their personal profile, so both need to be up to par. (Add-on services are a separate offering for you!) You are your own advertisement, so showcase your best work on your profiles and accounts! Remember that you don't need to be 'live' tweeting and posting. Look into becoming an affiliate for a social media scheduler such as Hootsuite (www.hootsuite.com). Take a look at a few others to make your delivery of stellar results to clients on your schedule and theirs: SproutSocial (www.sproutsocial.com) or the data compiler CrowdBooster (www.crowdbooster.com).

THE NITTY-GRITTY OF PRICING AND OVERHEAD

To demonstrate the value of your services, you'll need to decide on the matrix you'll use. For your clients, 'likes' don't necessarily mean more business. And, after all, your chief aim is to use social media to demonstrate how your client can grow their sales by outsourcing this marketing value-add to you! Some social media consultants require a retainer, making the hourly rate clear. Consider also providing a menu of services with three different tiers. Always include a time-frame because solo-entrepreneurs and small business owners want to know how soon it will be for their expenditure to convert to sales.

22. Gig King Or Queen: Reward Yourself!

THE IDEA

Temp jobs of the yesteryear included dusty offices where you had to register your details and call each day to see if any jobs matched your profile. So-long technology-void temping! Now, all you need is a profile and willingness to take on random tasks, that is, until you create a reputation in a specific skill. Feel the drudgery? Remember, temp jobs are exactly what they say, temporary. And with some great new apps, you don't have to go far. Cheer up! If you're a savvy shopper or musician, your hobby may just be your next paycheck!

GETTING STARTED

Plenty of small and big product companies recognize the importance of not only price-check verification but the value of being able to see precisely where their product sits on the shelf they're leasing. They need the eyes and smart phone cameras of app-driven temps. Think of it as modern secret shopping. You don't need to search high and low to find gig companies that connect the jobs with you, a gig shopper. Check out the Gigwalk app (www.gigwalk.com/gigwalkers). Once downloaded,

Gigwalk will show you a map of gigs local to you in real-time. Another app called Field Agent (www.fieldagent.net/) works internationally as well. MyLikes App (www.mylikes.com) allows you to endorse your favorite products or companies and get paid for the engagement resulting from your endorsements! If music is more your style, see what's available to play on Gigfinder (www.gigfinder.com). Another ever-growing platform for "Human Intelligence Tasks" is Amazon's Mechanical Turk (https://www.mturk.com/mturk/welcome).

THE NITTY-GRITTY OF PRICING AND OVERHEAD

On many gig sites and apps, prices are fixed, so you'll know how much you'll make before you do it. Gigwalk pays between $3-100, for example. Field Agents app pays on average $3-$8 and more if the job is challenging. (To get started, all you need to do is sync your PayPal (www.paypal.com) account to the app. It's that easy!

23. The How-To: Write That Book, Sell Each Chapter

THE IDEA

What questions do people know to come to you for their answer? Increasingly, authors are creating how-to books over a span of time, taking a single question and writing a short e-book for the answer. Take, for instance, Drupal. Maybe there's a very specific function you know how to create seamlessly. Why not take that question, answer it, and then take it to Kindle or other e-book versions? Taking a tour of Amazon, you'll see thousands of $0.99 authors doing just that! Then, once you have several chapters around a single topic, combine them into a single book with a higher price tag. By writing your 'how-to' in sections and essentially selling chapters one at a time, you don't need to defer earnings!

GETTING STARTED

For one week, keep a page open in your notes app. Every time someone asks you a question about something you know a bit about, or at least have an interest in, jot it down. Or just sit down for a brainstorming session. Here's a few questions to get you started on potential topics: *When you bought your last piece of technology, how did you know which one to choose, and how'd you research it? When you went on the European backpacking trip, how'd you know what to take, where to stay, and how to budget? In that last website rebuild, what new update changed the functionality of the site, and what shortcuts improved the back-end?* The only how-to books worth reading are the ones where the author has deep experience, right? Draw on yours, so that not only do others benefit from your knowledge, but you can monetize what you know!

THE NITTY-GRITTY OF PRICING AND OVERHEAD

By browsing Amazon's CreateSpace (www.createspace.com) or Lulu (www.lulu.com), you'll see pricing is pretty straight-forward. So, in order to capitalize on slim profits, you'll need to drive volume. Create a book launch group of interested individuals in the industry (programmers or developers, in the above example) or target demographic (think college graduates for budget travel, for example) who are willing to write a review. Send them the e-book for free and always be appreciative! Create a Facebook page, which will not only announce upcoming chapter releases but also add some levity to the topic with cartoons, etc. You'll keep your repeat customers looking for subsequent chapters and eventually the full volume. So, engage with them!

24. With The Right Insurance, Your Car Is A Money Making Machine!

THE IDEA

Whether you're in a city where a car is a convenience or a rural area where a car is a necessity, there are always some students who don't have one. It's called scarcity, isn't it? And when you hold a key for supply, there's an opportunity for profit. In this case, your asset is quite valuable, and the opportunity is to lease out your car hourly or daily to students who may need it for transportation to work, a shopping trip, or a host of other activities that makes the availability to rent your car a hot commodity!

GETTING STARTED

First things first, make a list of pros and cons of leasing your car to friends. Most importantly, should the worst-case scenario happen and you find yourself without a car, could you survive? Could you still get to classes and work while you were looking for a replacement vehicle? Once you've determined the reward outweighs the risk, review your insurance to see, in writing, that you have other driver coverage on your car. If you don't, get it. The additional cost per month is minimal. Then, find a free booking app such as ScheduleOnce (www.scheduleonce.com). You'll be able to mark times that you don't need your car, so that others can access your schedule and make a request for rental time. You approve it and send an email of where to meet for the keys. Sound familiar? It should because that's exactly what ZipCar does on a larger scale! But use your resources, your car. Next, it's time to start the marketing campaign. Think Facebook and word-of-mouth. After all, you want to know who is getting behind the wheel of your car.

THE NITTY-GRITTY OF PRICING AND OVERHEAD

Do your market research. Do car rental programs already exist near you? Price competitively but also gauge demand. Are students finding it difficult to rent through the bigger brand(s)? Do non-smart car or larger SUV options exist? That may be your market. To ensure you're paid, consider getting an online payment-processing terminal such as Authorize.net (www.authorize.net) or use PayPal (www.paypal.com). If your cash is flowing well, and you know a reliable handy-man, perhaps you needn't use your own car. Purchase one exclusively for renting or leasing out, but run your numbers carefully to see how soon you'd receive your return on investment.

25. Curtsy With Cuties: Etiquette Courses For Children

THE IDEA

Why not bring the nostalgic, polite days of old back creatively for those little girls who love dressing up? The pioneer of etiquette, Emily Post (www.emilypost.com), gave the gift of grace to thousands through courses, books, and more. But if you have envisioned in your mind dance cards, hankies dropped, and corsets, think again! As technology changes the landscape of what is socially acceptable and not, manners have evolved as well. Is it okay for children to play on iPads at a restaurant? Have they first put their napkin on their lap and said a polite "thank you" to the waiter for their drink? Parents can certainly guide polite behavior, but if you've talked with a mother lately, you might find she'd enjoy some support on the behavior front! We can certainly spot the person or child who is ill-mannered, impolite, and rude, and no parent wants that!

GETTING STARTED

If you have a penchant for etiquette and something caught your attention in the above description, it's likely you already know the basics. To refresh, take a look at etiquette books and websites and determine what's relevant to your girly audience! What key skills would parents appreciate that you could teach their children, for a fee? Once you have a topic outline, it's time to create your curriculum. Develop one theme per weekly lesson, building on the last, as repetition is key for children (and adults)! Consider developing a handout to send home with them as fun reminders, perhaps even with illustrations or coloring book pages. A six-week etiquette course, meeting each Saturday from 10 a.m.–12 noon, would offer a manageable commitment and enough time for parents to enjoy a Starbucks date while their children are occupied at the lesson! Remember: The decision-maker or paying client for your venture is the parent. And satisfaction for your fun course lies in both the assessment of the sparkly gals and Mom and Dad!

THE NITTY-GRITTY OF PRICING AND OVERHEAD

Just like gymnastic or ice skating lessons, price your course as a package. It's difficult to learn etiquette without consistency, so drop-in pricing is not ideal, except for guests or friends of your little clients. Scout out your location and negotiate with restaurant owners for a flat rate for food as well as private room rental. After all, at least one of your lessons will include table manners! Remind the restaurant owners of the benefit they will receive not only in a new host of well-mannered young patrons but the foot traffic from parents, potential patrons. Keep your costs lower by pre-booking for your next course. For example, if you are hosting a course April 15–June 1, get set for a week-long summer camp or your next six-week course starting June 15. This will allow for word-of-mouth to flourish, and you'll be seen as a permanent, reliable source for these unique lessons!

ABOUT THE AUTHOR

A bigail is an out-of-the-box strategist and connector when 'in her element.' Excited by the opportunity to talk about 'growing things' and expansion of all shapes and sizes, organizations and people, Abigail brings to partnerships something exceedingly unique: creative discernment. Said to be highly relatable, Abigail draws out commonalty in purpose whether speaking to large groups or one-on-one with stakeholders. Convinced that forward movement occurs only within a context of mutual trust, Abigail uses her 'connectiveness' to build profitable partnerships across finance and philanthropy, domestically and internationally.

Making Money the Millennial Way is Abigail's debut book. She has been featured in several venture capital and finance outlets online including her tongue-in-cheek letter published on Techli.com entitled, 'Dear Recession, Thanks. A Letter from a Millennial MBA.'

A truly globally minded individual, Abigail continues to apply her market acumen, international education and experience to various international development and finance initiatives through her firm

Sovereign Venture Advisors. As Managing Partner of 5th Avenue Acquisitions, Abigail sourced and cultivated the firm's relationships with Venture Capital funds, PEGs & healthcare-centric Investment Banks in order to offer medical and dental clients the financing solution to meet their goals. On the client side, Abigail sourced financing deals ranging from solo-practices to multi-group facilities, labs to medical technology firms across the United States. Abigail's consulting experience includes reporting in trust fund management at the World Bank, assessing micro-ventures for funding with the London- based HERA International in Georgia and Armenia, and business development support to various start-ups in South Florida and beyond.

Abigail believes investment is a function of both finance and personal time commitment. Abigail is passionate about international development and children, serving as a board member on three international non-profit boards. Through the Sovereign Venture Philanthropy Fund, Abigail centers both strategic and spontaneous giving on four pillars: trauma-focused healing programs and initiatives, women's micro-enterprise, bottom-of-the-pyramid familial agricultural initiatives, and Millennial literacy and education.

Abigail holds a M.Sc. Management from Imperial College Business School in London. Her dissertation on mitigating risk in BRIC growth strategy earned a distinction. She led a team of four in two entrepreneurship competitions, landing in the top five finalists in both. She graduated American University with a B.A. in International Studies, with a geographical concentration on the European Union and a functional concentration in public communications. She holds a Certificate in Central European Economics and Politics from Univerzita Karlova in Prague.

Abigail can be reached at:

Abigail@SovereignVentureAdvisors.com

NOTES

[i] Reed, Matthew and Cochrane, Debbie. "Student Debt and the Class of 2012." December 2013:The Project on Student Debt & The Institute for College Access & Success.

[ii] Federal Reserve Bank of New York. March 29, 2013: "2012 Q4 Quarterly Report on Household Debt and Credit. http://www.newyorkfed.org/studentloandebt/index.html

[iii] Louis, Meera. June 6, 2013: "$1 Trillion Debt Crushes Business Dreams of US Students" http://www.bloomberg.com/news/2013-06-06/-1-trillion-debt-crushes-business-dreams-of-u-s-students.html

[iv] Reed, Matthew and Cochrane, Debbie. "Student Debt and the Class of 2012." December 2013:The Project on Student Debt & The Institute for College Access & Success.

[v] U.S. Department of Education, National Center for Education Statistics. (2013). *Digest of Education Statistics, 2012* (NCES 2014-015), Chapter 3.

[vi] Brown, Meta, Haughwoutm Andrew, Lee, Donghoon, Mabutas, Maricar and van der Klaaw, Wilbert. March 5, 2012. Liberty Street Economics: Grading Student Loans. http://libertystreeteconomics.newyorkfed.org/2012/03/grading-student-loans.html#.U4o0kZRdUdE

[vii] Schawbel, Dan. September 4, 2013. "Why You Can't Ignore Millennials." http://www.forbes.com/sites/danschawbel/2013/09/04/why-you-cant-ignore-millennials/

viii Kurz, Christian. November 15, 2012. The Next Normal: An Unprecedented Look at the Millennials Worldwide. http://blog.viacom.com/2012/11/the-next-normal-an-unprecedented-look-at-millennials-worldwide/

ix Keeter, Scott and Taylor, Paul. December 10, 2009. "The Millennials." http://www.pewresearch.org/2009/12/10/the-millennials/

x History of Student Aid. Available at: http://www.finaid.org/educators/history.phtml

xi Name changed to protect privacy.

xii May 17, 2012. Pew Research Center: "College Graduation: Weighing the Cost...and the Payoff." http://www.pewresearch.org/2012/05/17/college-graduation-weighing-the-cost-and-the-payoff/

xiii Healy, Beth. January 29,2012. Boston Globe: "Domino's delivered for Bain." http://www.bostonglobe.com/business/2012/01/29/domino-delivered-for-bain-capital/kyMA0fIwPYvg2pa0UK1UfI/story.html

xiv Wilkinson, Bruce. *The Dream Giver.* Multnomah Books, 2003. (25.)

xv Fry, Richard. May 14, 2014. Pew Research Center: "Young Adults, Student Debt and Economic Well-being." http://www.pewsocialtrends.org/files/2014/05/ST_2014.05.14_student-debt_complete-report.pdf

xvi Proverbs 27:19, New International Version

www.ingramcontent.com/pod-product-compliance
Lightning Source LLC
Chambersburg PA
CBHW032003190326
41520CB00007B/338